L. M. Montgomery

Twayne's World Authors Series
Children's Literature

Ruth K. MacDonald, Editor
Purdue University Calumet

TWAS 834

L. M. MONTGOMERY

L. M. Montgomery

Genevieve Wiggins
Tennessee Wesleyan College

Twayne Publishers • New York

Maxwell Macmillan Canada • *Toronto*

Maxwell Macmillan International • *New York Oxford Singapore Sydney*

L. M. Montgomery
Genevieve Wiggins

Twayne Publishers   Maxwell Macmillan Canada, Inc.
Macmillan Publishing Company   1200 Eglinton Avenue East
866 Third Avenue   Suite 200
New York, New York 10022   Don Mills, Ontario M3C 3N1

Macmillan Publishing Company is a part of the Maxwell Communication Group
of Companies.

Library of Congress Cataloging-in-Publication Data

Wiggins, Genevieve.
    L. M. Montgomery / Genevieve Wiggins
        p.   cm. — (Twayne's World authors series ; TWAS 834. Children's
literature)
    Includes bibliographical references and index.
    Summary: Examines the literary career of the author of "Anne of Green
Gables" and the influence of her personal life on her writings.
    ISBN 0-8057-3980-7 (alk. paper)
    1. Montgomery, L. M. (Lucy Maud), 1874–1942—Criticism and
interpretation. 2. Children's stories, Canadian—History and criticism. I. Title.
II. Series: Twayne's World authors series ; TWAS 834. III. Series: Twayne's
World authors series. Children's literature.
PR9199.3.M6Z94   1992
813'.52—dc20   92-6201
                                                                              CIP
                                                                              AC

The paper used in this publication meets the minimum requirements of
American National Standard for Information Sciences—Permanence of Paper for
Printed Library Materials, ANSI Z39.48-1984.

10 9 8 7 6 5 4 3 2 1

Printed in the United States of America.

Contents

Preface

Only time can determine which books popular in their own day will continue to appeal to readers. More than 80 years ago the red-haired heroine of *Anne of Green Gables* captivated the reading public, put Prince Edward Island on the literary map, and refused to be forgotten.

Several works of fiction by L. M. Montgomery have remained continuously in print, and a recent revival of interest, sparked by television adaptations of Montgomery's works, has resulted in the appearance of all 20 novels in paperback editions. Surely it is time to forgive Montgomery for being a popular, female author writing primarily for children and to examine the reasons for her perennial appeal.

Only in the last two decades has serious critical attention been given to L. M. Montgomery. Early critics either ignored her or dismissed her perfunctorily as a dispenser of sentimental and idealistic escape fiction. A landmark in Montgomery criticism occurred in 1975 with an issue of *Canadian Children's Literature* containing eight perceptive articles that examined Montgomery's skill in satire, her portrayal of imaginative children, and her use of fantasy. The same decade brought a highly readable biography and two collections of short stories. In the 1980s came the publication of two collections of letters, two volumes of selections from the journals, two additional story collections, and a book of selected poems, as well as an increasing number of articles appearing in scholarly journals.

This book is the first full-length critical study of the works of L. M. Montgomery and the first extensive study of her work by a non-Canadian. I present this study with humility, not only because I am not a Canadian but because I am deeply indebted to the work of several eminent scholars who laid the groundwork for my research. Chief among these are Mary Rubio and Elizabeth Waterston, who supplied two invaluable volumes of selections from the journals as well as other excellent studies; Wilfred Eggleston, editor of the letters to Ephraim Weber; Francis W. P. Bolger, coeditor of the letters to George MacMillan and author of an important study of Montgomery's early career; Elizabeth Epperly, coeditor of the MacMillan letters; Rea Wilmshurst, who discovered and published a number of the short stories; and Mollie Gillen, author of a delightful biography. There are many others, too numerous to mention here, and my gratitude is great.

Librarians have been helpful, particularly members of the staff of the Robertson Library of the University of Prince Edward Island. Also, Sandra Clariday, Julie Adams, and other staff members of the Merner-Pfeiffer Library of Tennessee Wesleyan College have been generous with their encouragement and in the arrangement of interlibrary loans.

Funds awarded by the Mabel Pew Myrin Trust and administered by the Faculty Development Committee of Tennessee Wesleyan College made possible my research in Canada. Louise Trotter and Amy T. Turner assisted patiently, skillfully, and even enthusiastically in the preparation of the manuscript. I am immensely grateful to Ruth K. Macdonald, who proved to be not only an invaluable editor but a "kindred spirit."

Until I began this project, I had no idea of the number of persons, of all ages, who share my enthusiasm for L. M. Montgomery. They have cheered me on, and this book is for them.

Acknowledgments

Material from *The Selected Journals of L. M. Montgomery,* vols. I and II, edited by Mary Rubio and Elizabeth Waterston, and published by Oxford University Press Ltd., is reproduced with the permission of Mary Rubio, Elizabeth Waterston, and the University of Guelph.

Material from *The Alpine Path: The Story of My Career* and *The Poetry of L. M. Montgomery* is reproduced with the permission of Fitzhenry and Whiteside Ltd.

Material from *Rainbow Valley, Rilla of Ingleside, Anne of Windy Poplars, Anne of Ingleside, Emily of New Moon, Emily Climbs,* and *Emily's Quest* is reproduced with the permission of HarperCollins Publishers.

Material from the published letters of Lucy Maud Montgomery to G. B. MacMillan is reproduced with the permission of the Lucy Maud Montgomery heirs and of McGraw-Hill Ryerson Ltd.

All other material written by Lucy Maud Montgomery is reproduced with the permission of Ruth Macdonald and David Macdonald, who are the heirs of Lucy Maud Montgomery.

Chronology

1874	Lucy Maud Montgomery born, Clifton (New London), Prince Edward Island, 30 November.
1876	Mother, Clara Macneill Montgomery, dies; Maud taken to live with her maternal grandparents in Cavendish, P.E.I.
1890	Visits father in Prince Albert, Saskatchewan; narrative poem, "On Cape LeForce," published in Charlottetown newspaper.
1891	Two prose pieces and one poem published in newspapers; returns to Cavendish in September.
1893–1894	Attends Prince of Wales College, Charlottetown.
1894–1895	Teaches, Bideford, P.E.I.
1895–1896	Attends Dalhousie College, Halifax, Nova Scotia; earns first income from stories and verses.
1896–1897	Teaches, Belmont, P.E.I.
1897–1898	Teaches, Lower Bedeque, P.E.I.; grandfather, Alexander Macneill, dies; returns to Cavendish.
1900	Father, Hugh John Montgomery, dies.
1901	Joins staff of *Daily Echo*, Halifax, Nova Scotia.
1902	Returns to Cavendish.
1908	*Anne of Green Gables* published.
1909	*Anne of Avonlea.*
1910	*Kilmeny of the Orchard.*
1911	*The Story Girl;* grandmother, Lucy Woolner Macneill, dies; marries Ewan Macdonald; begins residence in Leaskdale, Ontario.

1912   Son Chester Cameron Macdonald born; *Chronicles of Avonlea*.

1913   *The Golden Road*.

1914   Son Hugh Alexander Macdonald stillborn.

1915   *Anne of the Island;* son Ewan Stuart Macdonald born.

1916   *The Watchman and Other Poems*.

1917   *The Alpine Path; Anne's House of Dreams*.

1919   *Rainbow Valley*.

1920   *Further Chronicles of Avonlea;* begins lawsuit against L. C. Page Company.

1921   *Rilla of Ingleside*.

1923   *Emily of New Moon;* named a Fellow of the Royal Society of Arts of Great Britain.

1925   *Emily Climbs;* begins residence in Norval, Ontario.

1926   *The Blue Castle*.

1927   *Emily's Quest*.

1929   *Magic for Marigold*.

1931   *A Tangled Web*.

1933   *Pat of Silver Bush*.

1934   *Courageous Women*.

1935   *Mistress Pat;* moves to Toronto; receives Order of the British Empire.

1936   *Anne of Windy Poplars*.

1937   *Jane of Lantern Hill*.

1939   *Anne of Ingleside*.

1942   Dies 24 April.

1974   *The Road to Yesterday* published posthumously.

1

"The Round of Life": L. M. Montgomery

The story of Lucy Maud (L. M.) Montgomery is the story of a sensitive woman and conscientious craftsperson who experienced joy and depression with equal intensity, loved natural beauty ardently, and pursued her writing career with indefatigable determination. It is also the story of a life filled with contradictions. She wrote lovingly of her childhood and youth on Prince Edward Island, picturing the island home of her "heart and soul and mind"[1] as an earthly paradise, but in her darker moods resented her strict upbringing and island relatives and neighbors, among whom she "found very few souls in common" with her own (*MacMillan*, 16). She loved both society and solitude. Something of a feminist, she was determined to earn her own living by her pen, but she could not discard the Victorian view of the supremacy of a woman's domestic role. A freethinker in religion, she taught Sunday school classes, was a church organist, and played the role of an orthodox and dutiful minister's wife. Her private thoughts were often rebellious, but she hid them behind a mask of conventionality.

The Island Years

Lucy Maud Montgomery was born on 30 November 1874 in the village of Clifton (now New London), on the north shore of

1

Prince Edward Island. Here her father, Hugh John Montgomery, ran the village store. Named Lucy after her grandmother and Maud after a daughter of Queen Victoria, she preferred the Maud but, unlike her famous heroine Anne, did not
want it "spelled with an *e*."[2]

When she was 21 months old, her mother, Clara Macneill
Montgomery, died of tuberculosis, and she was taken to live
with her maternal grandparents in nearby Cavendish, a small
farming settlement near the sea, "eleven miles from a railway
and twenty-four miles from the nearest town."[3] The Macneills
were proud that the family had come from Scotland in the eigh-
teenth century and were among the earliest settlers of the area.
They instilled in their granddaughter this family pride. According to a local saying, "From the conceit of the Simpsons, the
pride of the Macneills, and the vainglory of the Clarks, good lord
deliver us" (*Alpine Path*, 18).

Maud's grandparents, Alexander and Lucy Woolner Macneill, were "loyal, clannish, upright, God-fearing folk" (*Alpine
Path*, 19) who, in their fifties, having already reared six offspring, were assigned the upbringing of a lively and precocious
young granddaughter. They were rigid in their beliefs and customs, strict disciplinarians, and unsociable except with members
of their own extensive clan. Although well fed, well dressed, and
not unloved, Maud felt that her grandparents denied her
warmth and understanding and restricted her social life too
severely. The author's journals frequently comment on her
lonely and emotionally deprived childhood, a view that may
have been exaggerated by unhappy events in her later life. Still,
there was enough truth in this view to compel her to tell and
retell the story of a lonely, sensitive child dominated by unsympathetic adults.

The scarcity of congenial childhood companions helped to
shape her literary career. Solitary rambles in the woods and on
the shore intensified her innate love of natural beauty and
enabled her to describe the winding red roads, the encircling
sea, the mayflowers, and the spruce firs of her island with
details that gave her stories a strong sense of place. Her solitude
also forced her to seek imaginary companions and adventures,
and she early developed an "inner life of fancy"[4] so important to

the storyteller. Books supplied further companionship. Novels were scarce, but she read *Rob Roy, Pickwick Papers*, and Bulwer-Lytton's *Zanoni* so frequently that she knew whole chapters by heart. *Pilgrim's Progress* was another favorite, one of the few permissible as Sunday reading. Poetry was in greater supply, and she saturated herself with the lines of the nineteenth-century British and New England poets. She also looked forward to the monthly arrival of *Godey's Lady's Book*.

She could already read and write when she began school at the age of six, and the praise received from a teacher on her reading ability she declared to be "the first compliment I have any recollection of receiving" (*Journals* I, 371). She never forgot the humiliation of having to wear sleeved aprons and buttoned boots that set her apart from her barefoot classmates and later made this discomfort a part of the schooldays of her heroine Emily. At school she joined other children in making playhouses in the nearby grove, picking spruce gum for forbidden chewing in the classroom, and playing "Drop the handkerchief" and "King, King come along" at recess (*Journals* I, 380). Weekly attendance at the Cavendish Presbyterian Church was a social as well as a religious event. When she was seven, two young cousins, Wellington and David Nelson, arrived to board with the Macneills while attending school, and they provided three years of welcome companionship. At Park Corner, 13 miles away, she visited her Grandfather Montgomery, a kindly gentleman and a leader in island politics, and her Uncle John and Aunt Annie Campbell, parents of "a trio of merry cousins" (*Alpine Path*, 43) with whom she went trouting and berry picking.

Most of Montgomery's youth, however, was spent with adults, and she became a good listener. Her grandfather was the Cavendish postmaster, and visitors to the post office in the Macneill home related interesting bits of gossip. She also heard family and island legends recounted at clan gatherings, and many of these found their way into her writings.

She said that she could not remember a time when she did not write or when she did not intend to be a writer (*Alpine Path*, 32). She wrote descriptions of village scenes, accounts of school incidents, and biographies of her cats, using, like her heroine Emily, the backs of post office "letter bills" for these early

efforts. At nine she wrote "Autumn," a poem in the blank verse
of Thomson's *Seasons*. When her father, home from the West on
a visit, pronounced it be "very blank" (*Alpine Path*, 53), she
determined that her future verses would be rhymed. This
adjustment to the opinion of an audience, writes Elizabeth
Waterston, was to be characteristic of her entire career, for she
wanted recognition and approval as well as self-expression.[5]

By the time she was 12, she had accumulated a stack of
poems, which she hid from prying eyes. One of these she sent to
an American periodical and, after its refusal, to a Canadian
paper, with the same discouraging result.

A Year in Saskatchewan

After her mother's death her adored father spent little time at
home. But he finally settled in Saskatchewan, remarried, and
offered to provide a home for his daughter. In 1890, the 15-year-
old girl made her first railway trip, to Prince Albert,
Saskatchewan. It was a rapidly growing little town in which her
father, an energetic if somewhat unsettled man, was real estate
agent, insurance salesman, and auctioneer. Maud looked forward to a reunion with her father and a loving relationship with
her young stepmother. The restrictions placed on her social life
by her grandparents had become increasingly galling to the
teenager. Also, she hoped for better educational opportunities in
the high school at Prince Albert.

Once established in Prince Albert she continued to love her
father dearly and responded to the natural beauty of the western setting, but all else was a disappointment. She found her
stepmother domineering and hard to please and resented the
number of domestic chores, which included caring for two young
children, a half sister and half brother. High school was not
stimulating, and she attended irregularly because of her duties
at home. Hardly had she arrived in Prince Albert before she was
dreadfully homesick for Prince Edward Island.

Unhappiness led her to seek solace in writing. A 36-stanza
narrative poem, "On Cape LeForce," based on an early island
legend, was printed in the Charlottetown *Daily Patriot* in

November 1890, and she was intoxicated by this "first sweet bubble on the cup of success" (*Alpine Path*, 58). A few months later a prose article, "The Wreck of the Marco Polo," was submitted to a competition sponsored by the *Montreal Witness* and was accepted for publication. This piece described the grounding off the beach of Cavendish of the speediest sailing vessel yet built, a spectacle witnessed by eight-year-old Maud. In June 1891, another article extoling the beauties of Saskatchewan, "A Western Eden," was published by the Prince Albert *Times* and reprinted with favorable comments by several Winnipeg papers; during the same month the Charlottetown *Daily Patriot* printed a short poem entitled "June." There was no monetary reward as yet, but the 16-year-old author was beginning to receive some of the recognition she craved.

Returning to Cavendish after a year, she secured her grandparents' reluctant consent to prepare for the entrance examinations to Prince of Wales College. Her stay at the Charlottetown college was an enjoyable one, during which she experienced happy times with the other students and sufficient scholastic success to earn a first-class teacher's license in one year. While at Prince of Wales College, she also received notice of the acceptance of a poem, "The Violet's Spell," by a New York magazine. Her only payment was two subscriptions, but she was gratified, writing in her journal, "It is a start and I mean to keep on. Oh, I wonder if I shall ever be able to do anything worthwhile in the way of writing. It is my dearest ambition" (*Journals* I, 94).

Country Schoolmarm and University Student

A year spent as a teacher in Bideford, P.E.I., was a pleasant one. She liked her landlady, was successful in her teaching, and enjoyed the social contacts. Much of her time was spent writing and mailing manuscripts to periodicals, but nearly all submissions were rejected. Two unpaid acceptances from publications whose editors "evidently thought that literature was its own reward" helped her continue to believe in herself and in her ultimate success; she was determined that one day she would "arrive" (*Alpine Path*, 60).

A university course leading to a bachelor of arts degree was a cherished ambition but one Montgomery could not afford to pursue. She had saved $100 from her salary of $180 at Bideford, and her Grandmother Macneill's supplement of $80 allowed her to spend a year at Dalhousie College in Halifax, where she enrolled for a "selected course" (*Journals* I, 136) to further her intended career as a writer. She received little encouragement for this venture into higher education. Her grandmother consented and gave monetary support, but without any "real understanding" of her granddaughter's strange wish; her grandfather seemed completely uninterested; and her Cavendish neighbors and relatives expressed only a "somewhat contemptuous disapproval" (*Journals* I, 143).

Montgomery was inclined, like her heroine Anne, to exaggerate the pleasures of anticipated experience, however, and the year at Dalhousie proved to be another disappointment. She studied languages, history, and English literature; she received a "first" in most of her exams; and she reveled in browsing in the library and discovering new books. Despite the contact with scholarly minds and a wide range of reading material, 15 years later she wrote in her journal that her year at Dalhousie was a "waste of time and money" from which she received no "educational value" (*Journals* I, 390). The dissatisfaction that loomed so large in retrospect probably centered around the restrictions placed on occupants of Halifax Ladies College where she boarded, Dalhousie having then no residential facilities for women, and around homesickness for rural P.E.I. In 1895 Halifax was an urban center with a population of about 40,000.

The year in Halifax was a memorable one for her literary career, however: it brought her first monetary rewards. In the spring of 1896, she received five dollars from the Halifax *Evening Mail* for a humorous poem, another five dollars from Philadelphia's *Golden Days* for a short story, $12 from *Youth's Companion* of Philadelphia for a poem, and another $3 from *Golden Days* for a poem. Of this success she wrote, "Never in my life, before or since, have I been so rich!" (*Alpine Path*, 61).

She spent two more years teaching on Prince Edward Island, one at Belmont and one at Lower Bedeque. The year at Belmont was a hard one with backward, uninteresting pupils, an uncomfortable boarding house, and few congenial companions. Adding to her misery was an engagement to Edwin Simpson, a handsome second cousin studying to be a Baptist minister. Longing for love and a home, she thought she might find a satisfactory life with one "intellectually . . . more congenial" than other men she had met (*Journals* I, 187). As soon as she consented to the engagement, she regretted it; she was repelled by her fiance's caresses, and for 10 months, before breaking the engagement, suffered for the error of following "common sense" rather than "natural instinct" (*Journals* I, 188).

Personal problems did not influence her ambition. She rose early on winter mornings and worked in her unheated bedroom, wearing a jacket and gloves, in order to complete her quota of writing before school began. There were countless submissions and even several acceptances during the Belmont period.

The year as a teacher at Lower Bedeque was the year she was "possessed" and fell madly in love with a young farmer, Herman Leard. Despite a strong physical attraction of a kind hitherto unexperienced, she felt she could not marry a person so "inferior" to herself, one without culture, education, or any interests beyond farming (*Journals* I, 218). She described her dilemma as resulting from "a very uncomfortable blend in my make-up—the passionate Montgomery blood and the Puritan Macneill conscience" (*Journals* I, 213). Hot blood might have conquered cold conscience had not Grandfather Macneill's death carried her away from temptation and back to Cavendish.

When Alexander Macneill died, in March 1898, it was Montgomery's "Puritan conscience" that showed the young woman, then 23, the course to take. Her grandmother could not be left alone, so she gave up teaching to return to Cavendish, not gladly but staunchly. This was to be her home for the next 13 years.

Return to Cavendish

Back in Cavendish, she became "passably contented" (*Journals* I, 247) but felt herself to be a different person from the fun-loving, idealistic girl who had lived there before. However, she still thought Cavendish "the prettiest country place" she had ever seen (*Journals* I, 228). She attended church "painstakingly" (*Journals* I, 262), as well as the Literary Society, "pie socials," and a sewing circle; assisted her grandmother in the post office; and helped with the household chores. Two shattering events broke the even tenor of her days—the sudden death in June 1899 of the attractive young farmer, Herman Leard, and the death of her father in Saskatchewan from pneumonia in June 1900. Although their lives had largely been spent apart, she had felt her father "near and dear in spirit" (*Journals* I, 249), knew that he was proud of her and of her writing ability, and experienced an overwhelming sense of loneliness at his loss. In Montgomery's fiction, fathers tend to be either dead or geographically removed but are unfailingly sympathetic and lovable when they appear.

She found comfort and relief from monotony in books, her "faithful old key to the gates of fairyland" (*Journals* I, 262), reading both older novels like *Vanity Fair* and contemporary best sellers like *Quo Vadis*, rereading her favorite poets, and discovering a growing interest in history and biography. But her greatest comfort was in her "knack of scribbling" (*Journals* I, 249). At first, nine out of ten manuscripts were sent back by editors, but as she sent them out again, the number of acceptances grew. In 1899, she earned $96.88 from her poems and stories, not a great sum but more than half her annual salary as a teacher.

She left Cavendish briefly, in 1901, for eight months of employment by the Halifax *Daily Echo*, where she was the only female member of the staff. She felt the experience would be valuable to her career, and indeed this proved to be the case. She learned to work under the pressure of deadlines and amid noise and constant interruptions, discovering that "undisturbed solitude" was not vital to the burning of the "fire of genius" (*Journals* I, 270). Hired as a proofreader, she also edited society letters, composed a weekly column called "Around the Tea Table," wrote an ending for a serialized story, and trimmed another serial to one-third its original length. She continued her freelance writing, much of it "pot-boiling stuff" penned to supplement her $5 weekly salary (*Journals* I, 279), and some of it found its way into "first-class magazines" (*Journals* I, 270).

Feeling that her grandmother needed her at home, she returned to Cavendish in June 1902 and resumed her duties as household manager and assistant postmistress. Her determined writing efforts brought increasing monetary rewards, and editors were beginning to ask for her stories. In 1903 she earned about $500, in 1904 nearly $600, and in 1906 around $800 —quite a respectable annual income at that time. In fact, L. M. Montgomery may be termed, according to Mollie Gillen, Canada's first successful freelance writer.[6]

With little companionship other than that of an aged grandmother, she was often lonely and given to attacks of "the blues." Reading and writing helped, as did correspondence with friends, especially Ephraim Weber and George MacMillan. Weber was a homesteader in Alberta who had literary ambitions and who, in 1902, wrote a complimentary letter after seeing some of her poems in periodicals. Although he and Montgomery met on only three occasions, they wrote each other long letters over a period of 40 years. George MacMillan, a journalist, lived in Alloa, Scotland; his correspondence with the Canadian writer began in 1903 and continued until her death. They met only once, when she traveled to Scotland on her honeymoon. To these friends, Montgomery wrote of matters she could not discuss in Cavendish—her interest in psychic phenomena and in the theory of the transmigration of the soul, her rejection of the doctrine of foreordination and election, her questions about life after death, and her lack of belief in the divinity of Christ, although she held to the belief that Jesus was "immeasurably the greatest of all great teachers" and "sent from and of God as are all great teachers."[7] With Weber and MacMillan she shared her thoughts about books and poetry and details of marketing her writing. To find persons with interests like her own and to be able to discuss these interests, if only by letters, did much to relieve her loneliness.

She met Ewan Macdonald in 1903, when he came to Cavendish as the minister of the Presbyterian church. She became engaged to him in 1906, on the condition that their marriage be postponed until after the death of her grandmother.

She had no illusions about being in love with the Reverend Macdonald, but she liked and respected him. Convinced that any hope of "rapturous happiness" was a thing of the past, she decided to settle for being "reasonably happy" (*Journals* I, 322). The Cavendish homestead was to become the property of an uncle when her grandmother died, and she feared a future without home or companionship; she also wanted children. Ewan was an intelligent and educated man, a suitable mate, but she had some misgivings about becoming a minister's wife. In 1906, she wrote in her journal: "The life of a country minister's wife has always appeared to me as a synonym for respectable slavery—a life in which a woman of any independence in belief or character must either be a failure, from an 'official' point of view, or must cloak her real self under an assumed orthodoxy and conventionalism that must prove very stifling at times" (*Journals* I, 321). The words were prophetic.

The publication of her first and best-known novel, *Anne of Green Gables*, in 1908, brought unexpected fame and income, opened the way to acceptance of further works by L. C. Page of Boston, and, since *Anne* captured the hearts of numerous readers, promised public interest in similar novels. During the island years three other books were published: *Anne of Avonlea* (1909), *Kilmeny of the Orchard* (1910), and *The Story Girl* (1911).

In 1908, she also composed verses praising her "fair Island of the sea." "Island Hymn" became the official anthem of Prince Edward Island, but home duties kept her away from its performance at the Charlottetown Opera House. "The author and composer were called before the curtain and cheered," she wrote. "But only the composer could respond. The author couldn't go. She had to stay home and wish she could" (*Weber*, 87).

Her frequent headaches, nervousness, and depression probably came to a large extent from sheer fatigue. She not only published four books in as many years but, with her grandmother in her eighties, did most of the housework. She was now able to afford a servant, but she knew she could never win her grandmother's consent to such an extravagance. Almost as relentless in her performance of household chores as in her daily devotion of time to writing, she wrote to Weber with intentional irony: "I may have given up belief in foreordination and election and the Virgin Birth; but I have not and never shall be guilty of the heresy of asserting that it is not vital to existence that the house should be torn up once a year and scrubbed!" (*Weber*, 54).

After her grandmother died in the spring of 1911, Montgomery went to the home of her Uncle John and Aunt Annie Campbell at Park Corner and was married there the following July. A three-month honeymoon trip to England and Scotland followed, before she settled into the Presbyterian manse in Leaskdale, Ontario, and began her dual life as dutiful wife and homemaker and professional writer determined to be a "good workman" in the career of her choice (*MacMillan*, 3).

The Leaskdale Years

In 1910, the Reverend Ewan Macdonald had received the appointment as minister of the Presbyterian church at Leaskdale, 52 miles from Toronto, and of the nearby Zephyr congregation. The following year he asked for a three-month leave of absence since he was to be married to Miss Lucy Maud Montgomery of Prince Edward Island. Only when a parishioner produced a copy of *Anne of Green Gables* did he add, "Yes, I understand the young lady is a writer."[8]

Arriving in Leaskdale, in September, 1911, the 36-year-old bride found a small village of about a dozen houses and a two-story manse of white stucco over brick. She was disappointed that the house was built in "the ugly 'L' design so common among country houses," had no indoor plumbing, and was too close to the road for "solitude and remoteness." But it was her home, and she was its mistress, a satisfying experience for one who had "never lived in any house before where she had any rights and privileges beyond those of a dependent child" (*Journals* II, 82–83). The results of a flurry of renovation are recorded in her journals, which give detailed accounts of the final appearance of the rooms. In fact, numerous descriptions of interiors occur throughout her novels, reflecting the importance she attached to pleasant rooms where the furnishings are in harmony.

"I had never thought it a very enviable lot to marry a minister," wrote the new wife of the Reverend Macdonald, "but when I did it I made up my mind to perform as best I could such duties as are commonly expected of a minister's wife" (*Journals* II, 91). Members of the Leaskdale congregation remembered her as a gracious hostess, a welcome visitor in their homes, a witty conversationalist, and an active supporter of all aspects of church and community life who carried out her duties with "dignity and dedication" (Mustard, 4). Only to her journals—and occasionally to her long-distance friends Weber and MacMillan and perhaps to her beloved cousin Frederica (Frede) Campbell—did she confide her dissatisfactions with the role she so scrupulously performed. She found 9 out of 10 "pastoral visitations" to be "wearisome beyond description," particularly if she was required to feign interest in family photograph albums (*Journals* II, 91). Meetings of the missionary societies were "deadly dull affairs" in which she was required to "lead in prayer," a practice she considered a mockery of true communion with God (*Journals* II, 112–13). Often she must have felt in sympathy with Faith Meredith of *Rainbow Valley* who declared, "I'll never, never, *never* marry a minister."[9]

Motherhood, which she much desired, came in July 1912, just a year after her marriage, with the birth of Chester Cameron Macdonald. The next year she was pregnant again and gave birth to a stillborn child, Hugh Alexander, in August 1914. Her third son, Ewan Stuart, arrived in October 1915.

The adult Stuart wrote of his mother, "She was extremely sensitive, although an excellent dissembler, and though she experienced great peaks, she fell to great depths emotionally, which does not make for tranquillity" (Gillen, 1978, 44). During the Leaskdale years she lost her second child, a favorite aunt, Mary Lawson, and her cousin and dearest friend, Frede Campbell MacFarlane. Her keen imagination led her to picture vividly the horrors of World War I battlefields and the sufferings of the besieged and to dread what might be the future of the world into which she had brought children. She also coped with her husband's periods of deep depression, during which he was obsessed with the idea that he was not among the elect but an "outcast from God" who was doomed to a fire-and-brimstone hell (*Journals* II, 331). In 1919, a Boston specialist diagnosed his condition as religious melancholia, serious but unlikely to develop into violent insanity. His wife, determined to hide the truth of his malady from the rest of the world, suffered alone, increasing the frequency her own dosages of veronal.

Troubles with her publishers, L. C. Page of Boston, were an additional tribulation. In 1907, inexperienced and thrilled by the acceptance of her first book, she had agreed to the meager royalty of 10 percent on the wholesale price and consented to give Page the rights, on the same terms, to all subsequent books for the next five years. The binding clause was not only in the contract for *Anne of Green Gables* but in contracts signed for the next three books. In 1916, no longer committed to Page, she decided to offer a volume of poems to McClelland, Goodchild, and Stewart of Toronto as well as the Canadian rights to her new book, *Anne's House of Dreams*. McClelland was also to decide on the book's American publisher and selected Frederick Stokes of New York. Page threatened but did not file a lawsuit. The next year Page withheld $1,000 in royalties, claiming the discovery of a mistake in royalty reports. As a member of the Author's League of America, Montgomery sought the league's help, engaged an attorney to represent her in the Massachusetts Court of Equity, and won her case. However, she consented to Page's offer to buy entire rights to books already published by that firm, on the theory that "a bird in the hand is worth half a dozen in the bush" (*Journals* II, 285); this was a serious mistake since it cost her stage and film rights to *Anne of Green Gables*.

The Page company then announced its intention of publishing some early stories that had been in the firm's possession since 1912. Tired of the controversy, Montgomery agreed on the conditions that she supply revised versions and that the story collection omit references to her character Anne and any picture suggesting Anne. When *Further Chronicles of Avonlea* appeared in 1920 containing the original rather than the authorized versions and a picture of a red-haired girl on the cover, she again brought suit. The case was not decided in her favor until 1923, and since Page had filed a damage suit for libel and she demanded reimbursement for expenses, the entire matter was not settled until 1928, nearly nine years after its beginning.

Montgomery felt that Page was attempting to take advantage of "the average woman's fear of litigation" and of the fact that most authors could not afford the cost of a lawsuit (*Journals* II, 374). She determined to show that she came "of a different breed of cats" (*MacMillan*, 142). In her resolute defense of her rights she struck an important blow for the legal claims of all professional authors and one of particular importance for Canadians and for women in the literary marketplace.

Montgomery's years in Leaskdale were beset with problems, but there were also delights. She thoroughly enjoyed her young sons and found pleasure in her garden, needlework, cats, and books. Six periodic trips to Prince Edward Island were life-renewing events. There she gazed at the sea, which she missed in Ontario; drove the red island roads; walked in Lover's Lane, picked wild strawberries and spruce gum in the woods; lay on the sand of the shore; and visited old school friends and the Campbells at Park Corner. She would return to Leaskdale strengthened in spirit. Each time she visited the island, she felt that this and nowhere else was her true home.

Her flourishing career as a writer was another source of satisfaction, and the Leaskdale years were her most productive period. As well as writing for periodicals, she published nine books during these 15 years: *Chronicles of Avonlea* (1912), *The Golden Road* (1913), *Anne of the Island* (1915), *The Watchman and Other Poems* (1916), *Anne's House of Dreams* (1917), *Rainbow Valley* (1919), *Rilla of Ingleside*, 1921), *Emily of New Moon* (1923), and *Emily Climbs* (1925). In addition, the illegitimate offspring that she preferred not to acknowledge, *Further Chronicles of Avonlea*, was published in 1920.

In 1917, the editor of the Toronto magazine *Everywoman's World* asked Montgomery to write the story of her career. She modestly doubted that the story of a "long, uphill struggle" should be termed a "career" (*Alpine Path*, 9) but complied, and the result was published in six installments as *The Alpine Path*. She wrote mostly of her island childhood, early writings, and reaching her goal through the success of *Anne of Green Gables*. It is an optimistic account with no tinge of bitterness and no hint of the personal difficulties that she had faced and was still facing. The editor wrote that he was somewhat disappointed in the absence of personal material, particularly of "love affairs." The author was amused to picture the public reaction to a frank story of her life and replied that she was "not one of those who open the portals of sacred shrines to the gaze of the crowd" (*Journals* II, 202).

She continued to set aside at least two hours daily for writing as she continued to receive considerable public acclaim and was asked to lecture in Canada and the United States. In 1923, she was selected as a Fellow of the Royal Society of Arts of Great Britain, the first Canadian woman to receive this honor.

The Norval Years

The Macdonalds moved to Norval, Ontario, in 1925 after the recent formation of the United Church of Canada, which combined Presbyterian, Congregationalist, and Methodist churches. Individual congregations and ministers could decide on their own alliance, and the Reverend Macdonald, choosing to remain a Presbyterian, accepted a new charge, the small churches in Norval and Union.

Although Montgomery experienced some regret in leaving Leaskdale, where her sons had been born and where the people had been kind, she found Norval a "really lovely" place (*MacMillan*, 127). There was no sea, but the Credit River flowed behind the manse, and the hills were covered with pines and maples. No place could substitute for her island, to which she traveled periodically for rejuvenation, but Norval was not without its charms.

Household duties were somewhat lighter with her sons away in school, Chester studying law and Stuart medicine. The duties of a minister's wife were much the same as in Leaskdale and included directing plays performed by members of the Young People's Guild. When she received a disapproving comment that a scene in one of these plays was inappropriate for a performance directed by a minister's wife, she retorted, "Ah, but you must remember that it isn't the minister's wife who directs this play; it's L. M. Montgomery."[10]

It was the minister's wife who attended "Mission Bands, Missionary Auxiliaries, Ladies Aids, Womens Institutes, Sunday School Teachers meetings etc. etc. etc." and who sometimes felt so tired that she wished to hang herself on "the handiest gooseberry bush rather than go to another" (*MacMillan*, 137). It was L. M. Montgomery who kept alive her private world of the imagination and who published six novels while in Norval: *The Blue Castle* (1926), *Emily's Quest* (1927), *Magic for Marigold* (1929), *A Tangled Web* (1931), *Pat of Silver Bush* (1933), and *Mistress Pat* (1935).

It was more the minister's wife than L. M. Montgomery who coauthored, with Marian Keith and Mabel Burns McKinley, *Courageous Women* (1934). Written for young girls, the 21 short biographies stress their subjects' humanitarian contributions and intend to inspire young readers to show similar courage and dedication. Fifteen of the subjects are Canadian, and it is a valuable book, according to John Sorfleet, in its affirmation of both Montgomery's "Canadianism and her feminism."[11]

During these years she was rereading the classics—Gibbon, Macaulay, Trollope—while dipping into modern fiction, which she generally found uninspiring. The much-acclaimed *Strange Fugitive* by a new Canadian author, Morley Callaghan, she pronounced not only dull but disgusting since the writer's idea of art seemed to be "to photograph a latrine or a pigsty meticulously and leave nothing else in the picture." She considered herself a realist, for realism need not concentrate solely on the ugly. "Sunsets are just as real as pigsties," she said (Gillen, 1983, 161).

She was receiving fan mail from admirers, all of which she scrupulously answered. One letter came from 10 Downing Street. Prime Minister Stanley Baldwin wrote of his desire to meet her and thank her for the pleasure given him by her books, and she was invited to a garden party at Government House in Ottawa, where she met not only Baldwin but the Prince of Wales, later to become, briefly, Edward VIII, and his brother Prince George.

Ewan's poor health persisted, and he spent four months in a sanitarium in 1934. In the same year, the strain of worry and overwork brought a "little breakdown" of her own (*MacMillan*, 172), six weeks during which she could neither sleep, eat, nor work. In 1935, Ewan, unable to continue his work, retired, and the couple moved to Toronto.

The Toronto Years

Montgomery liked her new Toronto home, which she appropriately named "Journey's End." The Swansea suburb was like a country village, with pines and oaks, a ravine behind the house with ferns and wild flowers, the Humber River flowing by, and Lake Ontario within walking distance. The house was a new one with modern conveniences and was their own rather than a church manse. Of greatest importance was the fact that she could be with her sons, both studying in Toronto.

During the first Toronto year she was invested into the Order of the British Empire. She went to Ottawa for the ceremony and was pleased and excited but modestly wondered if George V had ever heard of his "trusty and well-beloved Lucy Maud Montgomery Macdonald" before he signed the citation (*MacMillan*, 176). She continued writing, producing two more *Anne* books and *Jane of Lantern Hill*. The *Anne* books, filling in gaps in the heroine's career not covered in previous novels, were written to please her publishers. She wrote *Jane* to please herself, as she had written *Anne of Green Gables*, and the result is one of her strongest novels.

In the fall of 1936, she spent a month on Prince Edward Island, still filled with its "old beauty" (*MacMillan*, 181) but under the shadow of a change. The Dominion government, planning a national park for each province, had chosen Cavendish, situated between two harbors and already a tourist attraction because of Montgomery's books, as the site for the P.E.I. park. At first she was saddened by the prospect, but when Premier Thane Campbell assured her that the brooks, woods, and lanes would remain the same, she saw that the government park would prevent the division of the farms into smaller plots and protect the area from overpopulation and from the cutting down of her beloved trees.

A main feature of the park was to be a farmhouse appropriately furnished as "Green Gables." This house, once the property of David and Margaret Macneill and later of Ernest and Myrtle Webb, was indeed used, in part, by the author for her description of Green Gables, but Anne's home was, like Anne, imaginary, and some of its description came from the creator's "castle in Spain" (*Journals* II, 39). Still, it was the site of Lover's Lane, the author's favorite haunt, and a place she visited whenever she returned to Cavendish.

Montgomery might, or might not, be amused if she could see "Marilla's Pizza," "Matthew's Market," the chain of "Green Gables" convenience stores, and the "Rainbow Valley" amusement park in the environs of today's Cavendish. Within the government park, except for flocks of camera-toting tourists, the pleasant rural atmosphere remains and takes us back to the author's "Eden of childhood" (*Alpine Path*, 45).

In Toronto, Montgomery's personal life declined. Ewan's health did not make the expected improvement, and she nursed him through a series of "attacks," not willing to send him to an institution and still keeping secret the nature of these attacks. Profoundly affected by World War II, she wrote, "It is unfair that we should have to go through this again" (*MacMillan*, 199). During this war she had the added dread that her sons would be called into service; Chester was placed in Class B because of poor eyesight, and Stuart was deferred as a medical student, but she still feared that conscription would eventually take her sons away.

In 1940, she wrote to MacMillan about a nervous breakdown that left her unable to read and about her burden of personal worries and anxiety about the war. Her last letter to her Scottish friend, in December 1941, contains the moving words: "This past year has been one of constant blows to me. . . . My husband's nerves are worse than mine even. I have kept the nature of his attacks from you for over twenty years but they have broken me at last. . . . Remember me as I used to be, not as I am now" (*MacMillan*, 204).

L. M. Montgomery died on 24 April 1942. Her body was taken to Cavendish to lie in state in the house now called Green Gables. Buried a few feet from the grave of her mother, in the old cemetery surrounded by the farmhouses, fields, and wooded lanes she had loved so well, she had finally come home.

2

"Born of True Love":
Anne of Green Gables

After eight years of growing success in writing for periodicals, Montgomery, in her own words, "went to work and wrote a book" (*Weber,* 51). In the spring of 1904, she began her account of a red-haired orphan girl adopted by an elderly couple, intending to use the story as a short serial for a Sunday-school periodical. Her central character soon became so real to her that she decided to follow a long-standing ambition and make the adventures of Anne the basis for a full-length novel. Written during the evenings at her grandmother's home in Cavendish, the work was completed in October 1905,[1] the handwritten manuscript typed on her secondhand machine that refused to print clear capitals and would not print a *w* at all (*Alpine Path,* 75). She submitted the novel to an Indianapolis publishing house, which promptly returned it.

After receiving rejection slips from four other publishers,[2] Montgomery put the manuscript away in an old hat box. About a year later, she took it out, reread it, found it still "rather interesting" (*Journals* I, 331), and sent it away again, this time to the L. C. Page Company of Boston. A letter of acceptance was received in April 1907, the book was published in June 1908, and the history of a phenomenal best seller began.

Montgomery found the idea for Anne in a brief entry in an old notebook where she had jotted down possible story plots: "Elderly couple apply to an orphan asylum for a boy. By mistake

19

a girl is sent them" (*Alpine Path*, 72). This slight theme does not seem a harbinger of literary success, but as the admirers of Anne well know, the girl who came to Marilla and Matthew Cuthbert by mistake was no ordinary girl.

After discovering her central idea and character, Montgomery felt that an acceptable book might result if she could "spread it out over enough chapters" (*Alpine Path*, 72). Such a plan indicates an episodic plot, a type of structure that strongly appeals to young readers. The incidents through which Anne matures and comes to terms with her environment, however, result in a plot that is more carefully structured and that has greater unity than may at first be apparent.

The book opens with a situation of interest and introduces the major themes. The first sentence contains a metaphor for Anne's life in her new environment: the brook near the main road of Avonlea "was reputed to be an intricate, headlong brook in its earlier course through those woods, with dark secrets of pool and cascade, but by the time it reached Lynde's Hollow it was a quiet, well-conducted little stream."[3] The tempestuous Anne who bursts on the scene in chapter 2 is impulsive and untamed: by the end of the book she has accepted the social mores of Avonlea and been accepted by that community.[4]

The first character the reader meets is Rachel Lynde, who typifies the strong work ethic of this rural Canadian community at the turn of the century. Mrs. Lynde is renowned for her efficiency as a housewife, and when cleaning and cooking are finished, she knits "cotton warp" quilts, awing her neighbors by completing 16 such masterpieces. In the Scotch Presbyterian community centered around the church, Mrs. Lynde is not only prominent in the Sewing Circle and the Sunday school but is "the strongest prop to the Church Aid Society and Foreign Missions Auxiliary" (*AGG*, 1). Moreover, Mrs. Lynde observes her neighbors closely and finds suspect any unusual activity, such as Matthew Cuthbert's riding out of Avonlea dressed in his best suit on a work day. Such interest in neighbors, typical of this closely knit community, can be both comforting and restrictive. This is the society that Anne is about to enter.

When Mrs. Lynde learns of the Cuthberts' decision to adopt an orphan, she expects the worst—houses set on fire and wells poisoned by strychnine. Although Anne brings no such catastrophes, she is indeed an element of disorder in the staid community.[5]

Another feature of the community, its insularity, is seen in Mrs. Lynde's distrust of any outsider. Marilla must reassure her that "Nova Scotia is right close to the Island. It isn't as if we are getting him from England or the States. He can't be much different from ourselves" (*AGG*, 7). This statement ironically foreshadows Anne's "difference" from her neighbors.

Thus, in the first chapter, Montgomery uses the time-honored method of the dramatist who establishes setting, whets curiosity, and prepares the audience for a character who will disturb the status quo (Rubio, 1985, 176). After this chapter, Anne appears and is immediately seen to possess qualities not valued or trusted in Avonlea—imagination, lack of emotional restraint, preference for beauty over usefulness, and power of self-expression. Five chapters present minor tensions between Marilla and Anne and a conflict between Marilla and Matthew, who is charmed by the very qualities that Marilla denounces and who wants to keep the "interesting little thing." This conflict is resolved in the sixth chapter when Marilla decides to accept Anne as her "duty" and to give her an upbringing that will teach her to conform with Avonlea expectations.

The following adventures of Anne extend episodically through 23 chapters and present intensified conflicts, such as Anne's outburst to Mrs. Lynde, the episode of the amethyst brooch, and the hair-dyeing venture. Through all these events, we see Anne develop and have a salutary effect on the adults around her. Gradually, as Anne becomes more restrained, the adults become less restrained, not only accepting but even appreciating her role in their lives.

Anne next achieves success in the world beyond Avonlea in seven chapters that describe her academic achievements and her career at Queen's College. In the final two chapters, Matthew dies; and Anne decides to remain with Marilla and save the family home, a commitment that makes her completely a part of her society, truly Anne of Green Gables.[6] Many incidents are self-contained and lend themselves to leisurely reading. As Susan Drain writes, contrasting the structure of the book with that of the television production, unity in the novel is "chiefly on the level of theme and character rather than plot."[7]

Some readers express dissatisfaction with the novel's ending, regretting the loss of the independent nonconformist who stamped her foot at Mrs. Lynde and cracked her slate over a schoolboy's head. But the ending is thematically appropriate. An orphan has sought and achieved a sense of belonging; such security demands both giving receiving. The rebel has conformed to the expectations of her society, but conformity is now less important to her than the responsibilities of mature conduct.

Although Anne's decision to place home and family before education for a career may not be the choice of most women of the late twentieth century, it is consistent with the view of women's role prevalent during the period in which Anne lived. Moreover, denying self-interest to promote another's happiness remains a viable option, even today. Also, Anne's decision is not seen as final (Rubio, 1985, 186). The metaphor of the stream in the opening chapter is balanced in the final chapter by the metaphorical "bend in the road." Anne explains to Marilla that the road that is her life no longer seems uncomplicated, leading directly to the fulfillment of her ambitions, but contains a bend that can only make her progress more interesting. The novel closes with Anne, rather than Mrs. Lynde, sitting by a window (Waterston and Rubio, 1987; *AGG,* 313), contemplating a world enriched by security and quiet happiness.

An Appealing Heroine

Of her first book Montgomery wrote, "There is plenty of incident in it but after all it must stand or fall by 'Anne.' She is the book" (*Journals* I, 331). Her judgment was correct, for, whatever strengths or weaknesses the novel may possess, it is chiefly the vibrant personality of the heroine that has made this story a favorite with children and adults for more than three-quarters of a century. What qualities of Anne have caused readers to take her into their hearts?

Anne has one of the greatest of all gifts, an enchantment with the beauty surrounding her, what Rachel Carson (and Coleridge before her) has called "a sense of wonder."[8] As she drives with Matthew toward Avonlea, she reacts with delight and awe to the blossoming trees and the shifting hues of the lake waters. Not even the disappointment of being rejected because she is not a boy can keep Anne from appreciating the "radiantly lovely" cherry tree blooming outside her window. Throughout the novel, Anne rejoices in the beauty of orchards, woodlands, flowers, brooks, sunsets, and the blue waters of the Gulf of Saint Lawrence. Like Wordsworth, Anne not only knows the "dizzy raptures"[9] inspired by the beauty of the world around her but finds nature comforting and healing. She can forget, for a time, her anxiety over entrance examinations by drinking in "the beauty of the summer dusk, sweet-scented with flower-breaths from the garden below" (*AGG,* 262). Her grief after Matthew's death is assuaged by the healing influence of "sunrises behind the firs and the pale pink buds opening in the garden" (*AGG,* 297). It should be noted that, in accordance with the philosophy of Wordsworth, it is usually the more mature Anne who looks to nature for solace and healing rather than for merely sensuous pleasure.

Anne not only responds to beauty but encourages others to share her delight. Marilla, Matthew, and Mrs. Lynde have been too occupied with scrubbing kitchens, sowing turnip seed, and knitting cotton warp quilts to notice the miracles of sunsets, white cherry trees, and fields of clover. Anne's rapturous flow of words may irritate or amuse the adult world, but her language points the way to a new vision and turns the commonplace into the beautiful. Avonlea has previously been satisfied with such names as "the Avenue" and "Barry's Pond"; Anne renames these sites "The White Way of Delight" and "The Lake of Shining Waters," not only articulating her own perception but reshaping the perceptions of those who hear her. Allan Bloom writes that "a new language always reflects a new point of view."[10] Anne instinctively recognizes that one interprets reality by naming it, as she says, "I read in a book once that a rose by any other name would smell as sweet, but I've never been able to believe it. I don't believe a rose would be as nice if it was called a thistle or a skunk cabbage" (*AGG,* 38).

The trait that Anne most values in herself is imagination, but she is unaware, of course, of the distinction between fancy and imagination made by the Romantics, chiefly by Coleridge. To the Romantics, what Anne terms *imagination* is really fancy or fantasy, the playful association of elements held in the memory to create in the mind situations that the inventor recognizes as unrealities, since fancy is controlled by the will.[11] When Anne "imagines" that her plain, serviceable dresses have frills and puffed sleeves, she is associating the glamorous garments that she admires with her own unadorned apparel, knowing full well that the two are not the same, that she will "just have to depend on Marilla" (*AGG*, 79) for any real change.

Anne's flights of fancy are her means of extending her experience. Her need for friendship is supplied by the fantasy that her reflection in the glass door of a bookcase is a real companion, and her longing for romantic adventure is partially satisfied by fancying herself a character in one of the melodramatic situations she reads about in popular fiction. Such inventions are comforting and generally innocuous, although they result in minor mishaps in the real world when she neglects to put flour in a cake or to report that a mouse has drowned in the pudding sauce. They are harmless and even enriching, as long as Anne realizes that she is imagining "things different from what they really are" (*AGG*, 55). She fails to make such a distinction when she becomes terrified by the fearful beings in the Haunted Wood, products of her own fancy. That incident helps her learn to maintain the boundary between fantasy and reality.

Anne's fanciful inventions endear her to children and adults who have had imaginary playmates or have dreamed of dwelling in marble palaces arrayed with velvet carpets and silk curtains. But Anne also has the more important gift of imagination in the sense in which the term was used by Coleridge. Through her imagination, she interprets the perceived world as filled with beauty and goodness and feels a vital kinship with that world. It is the "shaping spirit"[12] of her imagination that transforms an unexceptional rural village into a land of delight. As already noted, the language Anne uses to describe her surroundings is a part of her imaginative perception. Montgomery knew the transforming power of the imagination, writing in her journal of her grandparents' home, the Cavendish farm, as being "invested with a fairy grace emanating from my own imagination"

(*Journals* I, 121). Anne's invention of fanciful unrealities is appealing, but her imaginative creation of her own reality most enriches her life and the lives of those who know her.

A part of Anne's imaginative perception is her belief that the world is peopled with "kindred spirits," and she goes about seeking those to whom she may offer her love. She looks beyond Matthew's paralyzing shyness and verbal inadequacy to sense that he shares her love of beauty. She perceives that the honesty and loyalty of the mundane Diana outweigh any lack of imagination and intellectual distinction and make her a "bosom friend." Even Mrs. Lynde is eventually valued as a kindly soul capable of understanding Anne's desire for puffed sleeves. Not least among Anne's attractive qualities, then, is her loving heart.

Hungry for affection, Anne instinctively knows that the key to receiving love is to offer it, and so initiates loving relationships. It is Anne, of course, who suggests the "solemn vow and promise" (*AGG*, 84) that binds her in friendship to Diana. She impulsively kisses the sallow cheek of Marilla in spite of that dour lady's objection to "kissing nonsense" (*AGG*, 91). Even her mad leap into what she thought was an empty spare-room bed wins her the affection of the vinegary Miss Josephine Barry. But because Anne is a real child and not a paragon of virtue spreading unalloyed sweetness and light, she never succeeds in liking Josie Pye and nurses a wounded vanity that results in a long and unreasonable rejection of the proffered friendship of Gilbert Blythe. We love Anne for her virtues, but we love her even more because the author has allowed her some faults.

Although love may be strongly felt but uncommunicated, human beings need to be told that they are loved, and the ability to express the feelings of the heart is a mark of emotional maturity.[13] One of the several valuable lessons that Anne teaches the adults of Green Gables is that love can and should be expressed. Marilla and Matthew Cuthbert, products of a Calvinistic upbringing, have been trained to practice emotional restraint, to be as economical with words as with other resources. Their deep affection for each other is apparent but unspoken.[14] Marilla's first criticism of Anne is aimed at her outspokenness: "I don't like children who have so much to say" (*AGG*, 29). Although by nature more taciturn than Marilla, Matthew breaks the barrier of silence more easily. After Anne's performance at the school concert, Marilla admits to her brother, "I was proud of Anne tonight, although I'm not going to tell her so," to which statement Matthew replies, "Well now, I was proud of her and I did tell her so" (*AGG*, 264). Only the trauma of Matthew's death can bring Marilla to confess to Anne, "I love you as dear as if you were my own flesh and blood" (*AGG*, 297). Indeed, Marilla never learns the lesson of "a love that should display itself easily in spoken word and open look" (*AGG*, 238), but she has told Anne what Anne needs to know, a landmark in both their lives.

In a society bound by convention, Anne is a disrupting influence. She is the rebel, the nonconformist, the independent spirit who appeals to the child reader who chafes at adult strictures or to the adult who sometimes feels restricted by society's expectations. Because Anne wishes to belong to Green Gables and Avonlea, she is not consciously a rebel but, usually with the best intentions, manages to defy the narrow code of that society. Her garrulity offends those conditioned to believe that "children should be seen and not heard." Although Avonlea society, typified by Mrs. Lynde, considers acting "abominably wicked" (*AGG*, 222), Anne leads her playmates in an enactment of the fate of Tennyson's Elaine. In the Puritan society that distrusts novels, she delights in reading fiction and writing melodramatic stories of her own. She defies the temperance code of the strict Scotch Presbyterians when she unwittingly "sets Diana drunk" (*AGG*, 127). In a society that judges women on the basis of whether they are "good housekeepers" (*AGG*, 170), she flavors a cake with anodyne liniment and starches Matthew's handkerchiefs.

Marilla attempts to train Anne to conformity, saying, "All I want is you should behave like other little girls" (*AGG*, 85). The grateful Anne generally tries to comply, although it is "very discouraging work" (*AGG*, 160), and deliberately resists her society's mores on only three occasions. When Mrs. Lynde, who believes that it is permissible to say to children what one would not say to adults, criticizes Anne's appearance, Anne casts aside the pattern of the unfailingly respectful child and indignantly labels her critic "a rude, impolite, unfeeling woman" (*AGG*, 65). Well aware that any cosmetic alterations of the appearance are considered sinful vanity, she "counts the cost" before she deliberately dyes her hair, saying, "I thought it was worth while to be a little wicked to get rid of red hair" (*AGG*, 216). Rebelling against her teacher's unjust treatment, Anne refuses to return to school and play the model pupil. In most cases, however, she attempts to exhibit acceptable behavior, but her mind is her own kingdom.

Anne's ideas are often unorthodox according to Avonlea standards, and she expresses them honestly. In a society centered around the church and where ministers are sacrosanct, she finds the Reverend Bentley's sermons long, dreary, and unimaginative. Echoing Montgomery's own feelings, Anne questions the custom of public prayer, silently forming her own brief and sincere prayer of gratitude instead of listening to Mr. Bell's long petition and answering Marilla's protest with, "But he wasn't talking to me. . . . He was talking to God, and he didn't seem to be very interested in it, either" (*AGG*, 81).

Observing the stern, joyless approach to religion taken by faithful churchgoers, Anne feels that religion should be "a cheerful thing" (AGG, 171). She wonders why women cannot be ministers, questioning Mrs. Lynde's pronouncement against such a "scandalous" Yankee innovation (*AGG*, 251). The Puritan preference for utility over beauty[15] has little effect on this lover of the beautiful, who says of the road arched by blossoming apple trees, "Other people may call that place the Avenue, but I shall always call it the White Way of Delight" (*AGG*, 18). Marilla's ideas about plain, serviceable clothes, in sober colors and without an inch of material wasted, do not keep Anne from dreaming of flounces and puffed sleeves, and if thinking about clothing is "sinful" (*AGG*, 231), she is an unrepentant sinner.

Adults who wish children to believe that adults are always right and that their opinions should be unquestioningly adopted by children may find *Anne of Green Gables,* along with many other classics of children's literature, a "subversive" book.[16] Anne's fierce independence may even have political implications, for Elizabeth Waterston and Mary Rubio have recorded that authorities in occupied, postwar Poland attempted to ban the book (Waterston and Rubio, 1987; *AGG*, 308).

Setting

Eudora Welty believes that *"feelings* are bound up in place" and that "fiction depends for its life on place."[17] The charm of *Heidi* is inevitably linked to that of the Alps, and the Yorkshire moors to *The Secret Garden.* Not only did Montgomery create an appealing heroine, but she placed her in a clearly realized setting. Anne moves in her own special environment, a rural Prince Edward Island community located on a small peninsula extending into the Gulf of St. Lawrence. Montgomery skillfully inserts details of the community's appearance, its inhabitants, and their way of life into the narrative, so that the reader takes them into consciousness and acquires a strong sense of place. Marilyn Solt, in "The Uses of Setting in *Anne of Green Gables,"* collects a number of these details.

The first character we meet, Rachel Lynde, lives where the main road of Avonlea dips down "into a little hollow" crossed by a brook (*AGG,* 1). She lives closest to Green Gables, a farm located a quarter of a mile up the road at the end of a long "grassy lane bordered with wild rose bushes" and "barely visible" from the main thoroughfare (*AGG,* 3). The neat backyard of Green Gables is bordered on one side by willows and on the other by Lombardies. The house is "orchard-embowered," with cherry trees on the left and an apple orchard on the right (*AGG,* 3). Also on the right is a garden and beyond it a field that slopes down to a hollow with white birches and a brook. To the left, the sea may be glimpsed by looking across the fields that lie beyond the barns. Steps lead up to the front door, which, when open, is held back by a "big pink conch shell" (*AGG,* 298). By the door is a stone bench where Mrs. Lynde sometimes deposits her "substantial person" to share the latest gossip (*AGG,* 305). At the kitchen door is a red sandstone slab. Below the orchard, a lane that stretches "far up into the woods to the end of the Cuthbert farm" is used to drive the cows to and from pasture and to haul wood home in winter (*AGG,* 105–6). Dubbed by Anne "Lover's Lane," this path is a favorite place where one can "think out loud without people calling you crazy" (*AGG,* 106).

The only portion of the Green Gables interior described in detail is Anne's bedroom in the east gable, but the narrative provides readers with enough description of the inside of the farmhouse to visualize the life that goes on there. The kitchen, a sunny room with windows looking east and west, is the center of family life. Here meals are cooked and eaten, and, in the evening, Matthew sits on the kitchen sofa to read the *Farmer's Advocate* while Anne studies her lessons at the table. Warmth in winter comes from the Waterloo stove. Across the hall from the kitchen is the sitting room, which contains a jam closet where Marilla stores the raspberry cordial and currant wine that result in Diana's drunkenness. Between the two windows of the sitting room hangs a "rather vivid chromo" entitled "Christ Blessing Little Children" that causes Anne to have speculations that are "positively irreverent" according to Marilla (*AGG,* 56). Also on the ground level is the parlor, reserved for special occasions. Here tea is served to the minister and his wife and, near the end of the novel, Matthew lies in his coffin.

Matthew's bedroom is a small room off the downstairs hall. Upstairs are Marilla's bedroom, the imposing spare room, and Anne's bedroom in the east gable. When Anne first enters that room, it has "painfully bare" whitewashed walls, a "dark" four-poster bed, a table with a "hard" pincushion, and a window with an "icy" muslin frill (*AGG,* 27). Four years later the bare floor is covered with matting, curtains "soften the window," and the stark walls are covered with "dainty apple blossom paper" (*AGG,* 265), indicating both Anne's development into a young lady and her softening effect on the rigid life at Green Gables.

Anne walks past Mrs. Lynde's house to the church, center of community life. To reach Diana Barry's home, Orchard Slope, Anne walks down the sloping field to the east of Green Gables, over the brook by a log bridge, and through a spruce grove that she thinks of as the Haunted Wood. She and Diana walk to school by way of Lover's Lane and the Birch Path through Mr. William Bell's woods. The school is a one-room, whitewashed building with old-fashioned desks, each seating two pupils and "carved all over their lids with the initials and hieroglyphics of three generations of schoolchildren" (*AGG,* 107). Also in walking distance of Green Gables is the post office, which Anne and her friends "haunt" when the "pass list" is to be published in the Charlottetown newspaper.

Surrounding settlements are, like Avonlea, given fictitious names except for Charlottetown, capital of Prince Edward Island, located 30 miles from Avonlea, a half-day's journey by horse and buggy. When Anne first comes to the island, she is met by Matthew at the train station at Bright River, eight miles from Avonlea. On their memorable ride they go through New-bridge, a "bustling little village" (AGG, 18) where Anne first encounters the White Way of Delight. Apparently there are no stores in Avonlea, for the Cuthberts shop at William J. Blair's establishment in the small town of Carmody, which is a long walk or a short buggy ride from Avonlea. Five miles away by the shore road lies White Sands, which boasts a hotel with electric lights where American tourists sponsor concerts and have dinner in the evening, an unusual custom since dinner is the midday meal in Avonlea.

Avonlea is an agricultural community where Matthew plows in April, sows late turnip seed in June, and hauls potatoes "to the vessel" (AGG, 122) in October. Apple picking is another important fall event. Since idle hands are the devil's workshop, when women finish household chores they busy themselves with handwork: Marilla knits, Mrs. Lynde makes quilts, and Anne sews patchwork, although she prefers reading romantic stories.

The strong sensory appeal comes largely from visual images, but poplar leaves are "rustling silkily" (AGG, 22), frogs are "singing silverly sweet in the marshes about the head of the Lake of Shining Waters" (AGG, 161), clover fields are fragrant in June, and the "tang of the sea" is always present (AGG, 237). Anne tastes "yellow nuts of gum" (AGG, 114) gathered from the spruce grove near the schoolhouse and the "unromantic" dinner of boiled pork and greens (AGG, 101), and the abundant delicacies provided for the minister's tea, including Marilla's "famous yellow plum preserves" (AGG, 172). Montgomery tends to rhapsodize on sunsets, trees, and flowers, but in this book, most of the narrator's descriptions are brief and Anne's effusions are used as a means of characterization.

Humor

Anne of Green Gables, then, has an appealing heroine and a clearly established setting. It is also a very funny book. Anne's loquaciousness, Mrs. Lynde's curiosity, and Matthew's shyness are exaggerated qualities associated with the "humour" characters of Elizabethan drama. Montgomery uses another favorite technique of the comic dramatist that is related to the Bergsonian theory of the mechanization of the human—repetition by characters of their own stock phrases, such as Anne's "scope for the imagination," Matthew's "well now," and the "that's what" with which Mrs. Lynde closes her emphatic statements.

Not only is Anne's talkativeness extreme, but her bookish expressions are precocious and incongruous for the situations in which she finds herself. Her "highest ideal of earthly bliss" is to own a white dress (*AGG,* 16), and her red hair is a "lifelong sorrow" (*AGG,* 16). The discovery that she has come to Green Gables by mistake plunges Anne into the "depths of despair" (*AGG,* 26), but by the next morning she is ready to announce that, although her "brief dream is over," she has become "resigned" to her "fate" (*AGG,* 34). Anne's conversation is liberally sprinkled with such phrases, drawn from her reading of sentimental fiction.

The young Montgomery came from a family with "literary tastes" (*Alpine Path,* 15) and was an avid reader of the Bible, poetry, any novels she could procure, and melodramatic stories found in such publications as *Godey's Lady's Book.* Anne, however, spent her formative years with poor, uneducated families, was constantly occupied with housework and the care of younger children, and attended school regularly for only four months at the orphan asylum, where reading material was confined to schoolbooks. Anne, with her keen intelligence and retentive memory, has undoubtedly made the most of her limited opportunities, but her bookishness remains implausible in an otherwise credible story. Despite this problem of credibility, Anne's expressions are highly amusing, as is the bathos, or comic anticlimax, that occurs when Diana's or Marilla's matter-of-fact comments follow Anne's romantic outpourings.

Anne's speeches also provide dramatic irony when she misunderstands the language of others, as when she prefers one beau "in his right mind" to Ruby Gillis's desired host of suitors "all crazy about her" (AGG, 140). She is too ingenuous to use verbal irony intentionally, a technique reserved for the narrator, who inserts such gems as, "Mrs. Rachel was one of those delightful and popular people who pride themselves on speaking their mind without fear or favor" (AGG, 64). The phrase "without fear or favor" occurs in Kipling's "Christmas in India" and shows how Montgomery adapts quotations for comic effect, applying them to situations less heroic than those of their original context. For example, Hamlet's view of the world as "flat, stale, and unprofitable" is transferred to Anne's return to ordinary life after the glorious occasion of the school concert (AGG, 205). This device of the adapted quotation is used only occasionally in this book but becomes increasingly prominent in later works.

Montgomery is frequently criticized for her tendencies toward sentimentality and didacticism, and her first novel remains her most successful partly because she allows her characters to employ, for comic effect, exaggerated sentiment and fondness for moralizing, thus satirizing her own melodramatic tendencies. Anne, not the author, rhapsodizes over nature, and Anne sentimentalizes her situation as a "poor little orphan girl" in her amusingly dramatic apology to Mrs. Lynde (AGG, 73). Marilla indulges in excessive didacticism, being "as fond of morals as the Duchess in Wonderland" (AGG, 58).

Anne's expression "an epoch in my life" has been used by T. D. MacLulich as an example of Montgomery's satirizing of stereotyped and extravagant language.[19] "Epochs of our life" appears in Emerson's essay on "Spiritual Laws" and may well have been suggested to Montgomery by this source since she studied the essays and wrote of her admiration, with reservation, for Emerson (Journals I, 75). It is likely that the phrase also occurred frequently in popular literature. MacLulich notes its use by the narrator in Kate Douglas Wiggin's Rebecca of Sunnybrook Farm, a book with many resemblances to Anne of Green Gables and one that Montgomery may well have read since it was a popular publication of 1903. In Wiggin's book, Rebecca's first public prayer marks an "epoch in her life"; Anne uses the expression to denote her visit to the Charlottetown Exhibition. Thus, the phrase is used seriously in *Rebecca* but with humorous effect in *Anne* (MacLulich, 1985, "Heroine," 11).

Characters often find themselves in comic predicaments, which usually contain the irony of their frustrated expectations: Anne expects to realize her dream of raven-black tresses by dyeing her hair but produces a hideous green; Matthew expects to purchase material for Anne's new dress but comes home with a garden rake and 20 pounds of brown sugar; Anne expects to impress the minister's wife with her culinary ability but flavors a cake with liniment instead of vanilla. Mary Rubio has noted resemblances between Montgomery's use of ironic situations and Mark Twain's. In both Tom Sawyer's whitewashing the fence and Anne's apology to Mrs. Lynde, the child turns punishment into pleasure by outsmarting an adult.[20] Anne's apology to Mrs. Lynde results in the child's confinement to her room for truthfulness, while a few chapters later she is given the same punishment for supposed untruthfulness in the affair of the amethyst brooch, an inconsistency that makes an ironic comment on Marilla's child-rearing practices. In fact, throughout the book, the implicit question of just who is being "brought up" is raised, since Marilla changes more than Anne.

Not least among the treasures brought by Anne to Green Gables is the gift of laughter. Marilla is not without a sense of humor, but she believes that the world is "meant to be taken seriously." She is even "slightly distrustful" of the sunlight beaming through the window of her orderly kitchen (*AGG*, 4), a foreshadowing of the light that Anne is soon to bring to Green Gables. When Anne arrives, discovers that a boy was expected, and pronounces the mistake a "most tragical thing," a reluctant smile, "rusty from long disuse," mellows momentarily the "grim" countenance of Marilla (*AGG*, 69).

Autobiographical Elements

L. M. Montgomery was reared by dour Scotch Presbyterians, but, unlike Anne, she was unable to alter their rigid ways. Her Grandmother Macneill, she wrote, loved her but without the "slightest saving grace of understanding" (*Journals* I, 302), and her cranky grandfather bore little resemblance to Matthew (*Journals* I, 75). Yet the temperament and some of the experiences of the young Maud were much like those of her famous creation. Like Anne, she was sensitive to natural beauty, used her imagination to make "a fairyland" of her surroundings (*Alpine Path,* 47), and was fond of naming things, calling a geranium "Bonny" (*Journals* I, 1) and assigning names to favorite trees. She was also sensitive to language, thrilling to the phraseology of the paraphrases she was required to memorize, and composed several "lugubrious" stories in which "almost everyone died" (*Alpine Path,* 57). The adult laughter provoked by her use of big words remained a "bitter remembrance" of her childhood (*Journals* II, 40). A lonely child, she had an imaginary playmate, "Katie Maurice," who resided in the glass door of the bookcase in her grandparents' sitting room (*Alpine Path,* 74). Like Anne, she attended a one-room, whitewashed school surrounded by spruce trees. The "Haunted Wood" was a grove "in the field below the orchard" of the Macneill farm (*Alpine Path,* 74–75). The Avonlea locale was modeled on Cavendish "to a certain extent" (*Alpine Path,* 73), and Anne's year at Queen's, where she obtains a teacher's licence, resembles the author's year at Prince of Wales College. Montgomery's name, however, was fifth rather that first on the "pass list" for entrance into the Charlottetown college, and she won no university scholarship (*Journals* I, 91).

Montgomery, like Anne, was inclined "to rush to extremes in any emotion" (*MacMillan,* 19) but lacked Anne's resilience and became increasingly subject to periods of depression. Her strong sense of duty may be compared with Anne's, and she gave up her teaching career and postponed marriage in order to stay at home with her widowed grandmother. She did not, however, accept her duty with Anne's optimism but felt herself placed in an "awkward and unpleasant" position (*Journals* I, 221). The author clearly drew from many of her own experiences in creating *Anne,* of which she wrote, "Were it not for those Cavendish years, I do not think *Anne of Green Gables* would ever have been written" (*Alpine Path,* 52). But her disposition was darker than her brain child's, she suffered more from strictures against which she dared not rebel, and she had less effect on unsympathetic relatives and neighbors. Anne is the girl Montgomery would have liked to be.

The Orphan in Popular Fiction

Anne joins the ranks of female orphans who must make their way in an unfriendly world. This literary type may be traced back at least as far as *Goody Two-Shoes* (1766), the first significant book written especially for children.[21] Other examples of female orphans in best-selling fiction include Ellen in Susan Warner's *The Wide, Wide World* (1850), who lived in the country with a brusque aunt; Gerty of Maria Cummins's *The Lamplighter* (1854), a mistreated child of the Boston slums; and, of course, the heroine of Charlotte Brontë's *Jane Eyre* (1847), victimized by her cruel Aunt Reed. The latter has plenty of spunk, but most nineteenth-century heroines are remarkably obedient, and their stories contain strong religious elements, as in the stories about motherless, if not fatherless, Elsie Dinsmore, whose adventures began to be told by Martha Finley in 1867.

Although struggling orphan girls consistently remained favorite heroines, there were, according to Frank Luther Mott, two major "out-pourings" of such novels, the first in the mid-nineteenth century and the second in the first decade of the twentieth century, when *Anne* was written.[22] By the turn of the century, public taste wanted realism rather than religiosity, and charming, if not perfect, waifs converted their associates through their personalities rather than through quotations from the Bible. Shortly before the publication of *Anne* came *Lovey Mary* by Alice Hegan Rice (1903) and *Rebecca of Sunnybrook Farm* by Kate Douglas Wiggin (1903). Other lovable orphans later appeared in Jean Webster's *Daddy Long-Legs* (1912) and Eleanor Stratton Porter's *Pollyanna* (1913).

T. D. MacLulich has shown that Anne also belongs in the popular trend of the "literary heroine" that began with Jo March of *Little Women* (1868). Literary ambition, says MacLulich, was often used as a sign of the heroine's originality and her unwillingness to submit to all of society's restrictions. Although Jo

March and her most notable successors, Rebecca Rowena Randall and Anne Shirley, are outspoken, unconventional, and impulsive, they learn to curb these traits, assume nurturing roles, eventually marry, and confine their unconventionality largely to their writing (MacLulich, 1985, "Heroine," 7–10). They maintain the conservative domestic roles assigned to them.

Marilla belongs to the tradition of the rigid, crusty spinster who in most examples of the tradition is the heroine's aunt. Matthew is the kindly, taciturn figure (Avery, 17) who befriends the heroine. Mrs. Lynde is the stock busybody. These stereotypes are sufficiently individualized to have their own distinctive lives, however, and the lack of originality in the basic plot is compensated for by appealing humor and a strong sense of place.

International Acclaim

An instant success, the L. C. Page edition of *Anne* went through four printings in three months, and by the time of the author's death in 1942 there had been 69 printings. The initial royalty check, received by Montgomery six months after the June 1908 publication, amounted to $1,730, at that time a sizeable sum for the writer of a first novel. Since the author received 9 cents from the wholesale price of 90 cents, the sum indicates the early sale of almost 2,000 copies. Continued popularity is indicated by the fact that the Bantam paperback, first issued in 1976, had gone through 22 printings by 1986.

Montgomery reported to Ephraim Weber the receipt of copies of 60 reviews, all but five laudatory (*Weber,* 71). She was particularly pleased by the complimentary review of the London *Spectator* and was thrilled by a letter from Mark Twain, who pronounced Anne to be "the dearest and most lovable child in fiction since the immortal Alice."[24] Modern critics cannot deny the book's continuing appeal. For example, Sheila Egoff, while consigning Montgomery to the "heavily sentimental 'sweetness and light' school of writing for children," admits that "to denigrate the literary qualities of *Anne of Green Gables* is as useless an exercise as carping about the architecture of the National War Memorial. Anne arrived and she has stayed."[25]

From the Canadian Maritimes, *Anne* has crossed national boundaries to become an international best seller. Five English editions had appeared by May 1909; by 1912 Anne had been translated into Swedish, Dutch, and Polish; and the book now appears in at least 16 languages other than English.[26] Astrid Lindgren, the Swedish author of *Pippi Longstocking*, has acknowledged her debt to Montgomery,[27] and *Anne* has enjoyed tremendous popularity in Poland. First appearing there in 1912 when Poland was divided between three world powers, *Anne* was warmly welcomed as a book that stressed qualities needed by the Poles in order to survive as a people.[28] Its continued popularity is vouched for by its appearance in 1965 on a list of favorite books of students in Polish secondary schools and by the selection in 1982 of L. M. Montgomery by a magazine for adolescents as the second-favorite author of Polish youth. Between 1948 and 1982 the books about Anne appeared in 39 editions in Poland with the number of copies sold totaling over 2 million (Wachowicz, 17–22). A stage production of *Anne of Green Gables* has enjoyed the longest continuous run of any play in the history of Polish theater. A 90-year-old Polish woman writes of being sent to Siberia as a young girl when her family was suspected of participation in the underground independence movement. She took with her into exile her three "most precious" possessions: photographs of her dead parents, a book by Adam Mickiewicz, and her copy of *Anne of Green Gables* (Wachowicz, 26).

Since 1952, when *Anne* was first translated into Japanese as *Akage no An* (Anne of the Red Hair), at least 16 editions have been produced by Japanese publishers, who have also furnished cookbooks and handicraft books with the Anne motif as well as books about Prince Edward Island. Yuko Katsura reports that *Anne,* which has sold over 1 million copies in Japan, is particularly popular with Japanese girls of junior-high-school age, many of whom continue to read Montgomery books into adulthood, becoming lifelong devotees.[29] The largest Montgomery fan club, "Buttercups," has a membership of over 300. Tours to Prince Edward Island, arranged by Japanese publishers, attract thousands of participants annually.

Several possibilities may be advanced as reasons for this tremendous appeal in Japan. Japanese women, living under strict conventions in a male-dominated environment, find Anne's independent spirit attractive but, at the same time, are drawn to her love of home and family, a quality particularly important in Japanese society. Charmaine Gaudet feels that in possessing these two traits Anne perhaps embodies "both what the Japanese are and what many wish they could be."[30] Anne also loves natural beauty, as do the Japanese, and her life in a pastoral setting allows readers a vicarious escape from crowded, industrialized Japan. Doubtless Anne's success in school is valued by young people in a society that emphasizes academic achievement, and her troubles with geometry may comfort those experiencing problems with the demanding Japanese curriculum. That Anne becomes a leader in Avonlea, makes her guardians proud of her, and does as well as Gilbert in school, all in spite of the fact that she is not the expected boy, pleases young girls everywhere but perhaps especially Japanese females. At any rate, a young Tokyo publisher, Jichio Kondo, writes that "the way many Japanese feel about Anne, Montgomery, and the island is almost a religion. In this religion, Anne is the saint, Green Gables the cathedral, and the trip (to P.E.I.) is a pilgrimage" (Gaudet, 10).

Not only has Anne crossed national boundaries, but she has bridged the generation gap. Montgomery was herself amazed by the interest adults displayed in Anne. To her cousin Murray Macneill she wrote, "It has been a great surprise to me that Anne should have taken so well with 'grown-ups.' When I wrote it I thought is would be an amusing and harmless tale for Sunday School libraries and 'kiddies,' but I did not suppose it would appeal to older readers."[31] Children are captivated by Anne's humorous adventures and identify with the child who, in spite of good intentions, finds herself embroiled in difficulties that shock the adult world. The fairy-tale element of the story in which an ugly duckling becomes a swan also has a special attraction for the young. Adolescents identify with Anne's rebellion against social restrictions, her intense response to experience, and her desire to belong while maintaining her own identity (Rubio, 1985, 173). The suggestion of a future romance with Gilbert is satisfying to adolescent readers who are both intrigued and frightened by sexuality (Waterston, 1975, 25). Anne's role reversal, in which she nurtures Marilla, enacts a fantasy that, according to Freud, is common to adolescence, a period when the young seek to assume active rather than passive roles.[32]

Young readers enjoy the tension between child and adults, but mature readers appreciate the full significance of the struggles between beauty and utility, imagination and strict practicality, truth and propriety, and love and obedience. The adult who has not forgotten childhood identifies with and rejoices in Anne, but, at the same time, understands the loneliness of Marilla's and Matthew's convention-bound existence and their need for Anne's insights. It is significant that the point of view in the novel is more often that of Marilla than of Anne.

Anne on Stage and Screen

Anne has also gone beyond the print medium to the stage and to both the large and small screen. Within the author's lifetime, the novel became the basis for two three-act plays and two movies. After a lawsuit against L. C. Page in 1915, Montgomery agreed to a settlement of $17,880, losing the rights to her first seven novels. Page then sold the screen rights to *Anne* for $40,000. Not only did the author receive no profit from the adaptations, but she had no control over their content. The 1919 silent film she judged "well photographed" but found Mary Miles Mintner not "gingery" enough for Anne and resented the lack of Prince Edward Island atmosphere, especially the appearance in the film of an American flag and a skunk, an animal then unknown to the island. She fumed at such "crass, blatant Yankeeism" (*Journals* II, 373).

She was more pleased with the 1934 "talkie," which she saw four times, but still had reservations. Two scenes were filmed on Prince Edward Island, but the remainder was "pure California." Anne Shirley, who had changed her stage name from Dawn O'Day to that of the title character, was rather good but lacked a certain "elfin charm," and Diana and Gilbert were unsatisfactory. Helen Westley would have been better cast as Mrs. Lynde than as Marilla, and the blending of Mrs. Lynde and Mrs. Barry into one character was a puzzling innovation (*MacMillan,* 179). It is surprising that the author accepted the R.K.O. production as well as she did, considering the drastic changes made in the plot and in the protagonist. Anne is older, 14, when she arrives at Green Gables, and the major emphasis is placed on the romance with Gilbert, with whom Anne flirts rather shamelessly, offering to kiss him rather than spurning him in the scene in which he rescues her from the sinking barge. The hair-dyeing episode is omitted, along with certain other escapades, and a complication is invented in which Marilla and Matthew oppose Anne's alliance with Gilbert because Gilbert's father robbed Matthew of the girl he loved. This situation is sentimentally resolved by Gilbert's securing a renowned doctor to save the life of the ailing Matthew.

The popularity in Poland of a dramatic version of *Anne* has already been mentioned. A musical written and composed by Don Harron and Norman Campbell was first performed at the opening of the Charlottetown Confederation Centre for the Arts in 1965; it has since toured Canada and abroad, received the Musical of the Year Award from London critics in 1969, and been part of Canada's contribution to the World Exposition in Japan in 1970. Now in its twenty-sixth year, the musical plays to capacity audiences every summer in Charlottetown.

An award-winning television miniseries, produced by Kevin Sullivan for the Canadian Broadcasting Corporation and subsequently aired in the United States and 39 other countries,[33] has resulted in renewed and wider popularity for Canada's most renowned heroine. The television film has strong visual appeal; Megan Follows is believable, if a bit too impudent, as Anne; and Colleen Dewhurst blends austerity and humor in her superb portrayal of Marilla. Structural changes, however, give the film a different focus from that of the novel. The book begins by emphasizing the community of which Anne is to become a part, whereas the film opens with Anne's hard life as a foster child and as an orphanage inmate, thus sentimentalizing her plight far more than is the case in the original work. After Anne's arrival at Green Gables, her film adventures are divided into two major sections: first, the trial period, which promotes suspense through the uncertainty of Anne's acceptance by Marilla; and, second, the love story, in which a series of conflicts between Anne and Gilbert culminates in their happy relationship.

In the novel there is no lengthy trial period, for Anne is told that she may stay at Green Gables on the second day after her arrival; it is not her literal but her psychological acceptance that is in question, a more complex problem. After the trial period, comprising approximately one-third of the film, the focus shifts to the Anne-Gilbert relationship. Far more prominent than in the novel, Gilbert plays a part in several episodes from which he is absent in the original. For example, he appears at the Sunday School picnic in athletic rivalry with Anne; the hair-dying episode is placed immediately after the scene in which he calls Anne "Carrots," so that he becomes the motivating force behind the disaster; and it is his taunting presence that causes Anne to accept the dare to climb the ridgepole. While a few episodes, such as Anne's attempt at a Christmas dance to show her control over Gilbert, are inventions of the screenwriters, most events are drawn from the novel but adapted to the romance theme. Thus, in the film Gilbert becomes a unifying element for the novel's episodic plot, but the result is a sacrifice of complexity and depth. Susan Drain, who has provided a detailed analysis of the television adaptation, concludes: "Beautiful and moving as it is, the film is yet a lesser accomplishment. It succeeds by reducing to predictability the leisurely complexities of character development and the gradual accommodation of individual and community that are the deeper patterns of Montgomery's original. . . . The film is exquisite romance, but the novel is a *Bildungsroman*" (Drain, 1987, 64, 72).

Anne of Green Gables has several levels of appeal. It is a story of a child's progress toward maturity, of an isolate's search for belonging, of the shaping power of the imagination, and an appealing child's power to transform. It contains mythic and fairy-tale elements, is rich in humor, and, through its portrayal of Canadian rural life at the turn of the century, is valuable as social history. It offers immediate appeal to children and adolescents and continues to delight adults. It is also a specimen of Montgomery's "real style" (*MacMillan,* 44), since she wrote this book solely to please herself, not to cater to public taste. In August 1907, before the appearance of the published work, she wrote in her journal: "The book may or may not sell well. I wrote it for love, not money—but very often such books are the most successful—just as everything in life that is born of true love is better than something constructed for mercenary ends" (*Journals* I, 331).

3

From Avonlea to Four Winds:
1909–1917

The gratifying response of readers to *Anne of Green Gables* led the L. C. Page Company to urge Montgomery to complete a second book about the popular young redhead. In June 1908, Montgomery wrote in her journal, "*Anne* is already in her second edition. My publishers are hurrying me now for the sequel" (*Journals* I, 335–36).

Series books steadily gained popularity with young readers from the time of the *Rollo* series of Jacob Abbott in the 1830s. Louisa May Alcott followed her popular *Little Women* with the sequels *Little Men* and *Jo's Boys*, and Mark Twain carried Tom Sawyer through further adventures. The success of the first best seller of the twentieth century, Alice Megan Rice's *Mrs. Wiggs of the Cabbage Patch* (1901), led its author to compose a sequel, *Lovey Mary* (1903), and Kate Douglas Wiggin followed her *Rebecca of Sunnybrook Farm* (1903) with *New Chronicles of Rebecca* (1907). These are only a few examples of popular characters whose adventures continued in later books. Young readers are insatiable in their appetite for stories of the Bobbsey Twins, Nancy Drew, the Hardy Boys, the Five Peppers, and many other series characters. Sequels answer a favorite question of children at the end of a story, "What happened next?" For publishers, a sequel to a popular book is an assurance of another moneymaker.

Montgomery, anxious to further her career and delighted by the acceptance of her first book, hastened to comply with her publishers' request, but not without misgivings. "I'm working at it," she wrote in her journal, "but it will not be as good as *Green Gables*. I have to force it" (*Journals* I, 336).

Anne of Avonlea

During the summer of 1907, Montgomery planned her first Anne sequel, *Anne of Avonlea*. The preliminary work consisted of "collecting material for it, blocking out chapters, devising incidents and fitting them into each other, and 'brooding' up the characters" (*Journals* I, 332). After almost a full year of writing and revision, the manuscript was completed in the late summer of 1908. Then came the typing, an "excessively wearisome" task consuming three or four hours each day (*Weber*, 70). The manuscript was mailed to Page in November 1908 and publication completed in September 1909.

As has been noted, Montgomery spent considerable time in "blocking out chapters." The result is a carefully structured book; indeed, Montgomery felt that it may have been too carefully structured. She wrote to Ephraim Weber, "There seems to be more of a 'made to order' flavour about it and less of spontaneity. . . . It didn't *grow* as the first book did. I simply *built* it" (*Weber*, 61, 74).

Montgomery "built" a plot containing seven threads: Anne's career as the Avonlea schoolteacher; her contributions to the Avonlea Village Improvement Society; her involvement with the young twins adopted by Marilla; her acquaintance with a crusty neighbor, Mr. James A. Harrison; her playing hostess to a famous author, Mrs. Charlotte E. Morgan; her promotion of the reunion of Miss Lavendar Lewis with a long-estranged lover; and her growing friendship with Gilbert Blythe. The opening chapter introduces six of these seven plot elements, all except Anne's interest in Mrs. Morgan. Thereafter, each chapter focuses primarily on one of the elements with others interwoven.

Anne serves for two years as the schoolmistress in Avonlea's one-room schoolhouse, whose building and activities are similar to those experienced by the author as a pupil in the Cavendish school and as a teacher in Bideford, Belmont, and Lower Bedeque. She knew both the delights and the frustrations of being the village schoolmarm. Anne particularly enjoys her pupils' humorous remarks and distinctive personalities. One of her students is the imaginative Paul Irving, whose flights of fancy mirror those of the younger Anne but are less convincing. A 10-year-old boy who claims to know imaginary "rock people" and to have sailed to the sunset in an enchanted boat[1] lacks credibility. Since Paul is to become the stepson of Lavendar Lewis, however, he prepares the reader for the Miss Lavendar plot thread, the principal focus of the last part of the book.

The major frustration of Anne's teaching career is her failure to win the respect of young Anthony Pye, a mischievous boy who considers female teachers to be inferior to males. Anne's encounters with such prejudice reflect Montgomery's own experiences in a profession long controlled by men. The teachers' college at Charlottetown, P.E.I., was founded in 1856 but did not admit women until 1879, and the young Montgomery did not encounter a female teacher until the age of 12.[2] A second female teacher in Cavendish, Hattie Gordon, became a role model for the young Maud and the basis for the fictional character of Muriel Stacey in *Anne of Green Gables*. *Anne of Avonlea* is dedicated to Hattie Gordon Smith.

Anne begins her teaching career with "rose-tinted ideals" (*AA*, 2) of the proper methods for developing the good in every child, but her dreams soon adjust to reality. Her opposition to corporal punishment, considered by her contemporaries necessary to maintain discipline, collapses on a particularly frustrating day in the schoolroom, and she whips Anthony Pye. The explosion of firecrackers in the schoolroom stove on this "Jonah day" (*AA*, 122) parallels the shattering of Anne's idealistic views of the life of a teacher (Waterston and Rubio, 1987; *AA*, 281).[3]

Anne seeks to improve not only her pupils but the physical aspects of her community. Landscape design and village beautification were advocated by articles in popular magazines of the period (Waterston and Rubio, 1987; *AA*, 278). Influenced by this trend as well as by her own love of beauty, Anne becomes, in a second plot thread, a founder and enthusiastic member of the

Avonlea Village Improvement Society. As with her educational theories, her views on community improvement are generally sound and commendable, but idealism comes to be tempered by the realities of the human condition. Comic obstacles plague the path of Anne and her fellow "improvers." Reluctant to be improved, several villagers ridicule the society's aims, Mr. Lawrence Bell remarking that he would "whitewash his barns if nothing else would please them but he would not hang lace curtains in his cowstable windows" (*AA*, 54). Mrs. Rachel Lynde distrusts any idea originating in "some rubbishy Yankee magazine" (*AA*, 13). Through the mistake of a local painter, the village hall is painted a brilliant blue. The society succeeds in preventing a farmer from renting his fence to be painted with patent medicine advertisements only through Anne's accidental discovery of his political corruption. Another "explosion" both impedes and assists the progress of the improvers: a violent storm levels young trees planted by the society but also destroys Levi Boulter's old house, an eyesore removed not by the earnest efforts of Anne and her associates but by an act of nature (Waterston and Rubio, 1987; *AA*, 278).

In a third plot element, a series of minor explosions accompanies the introduction into Green Gables life of the orphaned twins, Davy and Dora. Davy is the mischievous "bad boy," a type already popularized by Mark Twain, Thomas Bailey Aldrich, and others. Dora is the prim and proper model child, approved by Avonlea society but considered less interesting than her brother even by such models of rectitude as Marilla and Mrs. Lynde.

Like the younger Anne, Davy has a series of comic escapades and misunderstandings of adult concepts and language, with ironic results. One of the most memorable examples of the latter is found in Davy's belief that there will be plenty of jam in heaven because of the catechism's statement that God "makes preserves and redeems us" (*AA*, 150).

In creating the contrasting twins, Montgomery may be revealing, consciously or subconsciously, her own dissatisfaction with gender roles in Cavendish society (Waterston and Rubio, 1987; *AA*, 278). Energetic and adventure-loving like Davy, she must have longed to disrupt the smooth, and often monotonous, surface of village life. Davy creates a sensation during a church service by dropping a caterpillar down the neck of the placid and irreproachable Lauretta White. While Dora industriously shells peas, Davy turns the pods into boats with matchstick masts. Davy's creativity and imagination are qualities shared by Maud Montgomery, but Cavendish society expected her to be content with a domestic role as a sheller of peas.

The 16-year-old Anne has retained some of her childish impulsiveness, which leads her to the comic mistake of selling Mr. James A. Harrison's Jersey cow instead of her own. Her error is forgiven by her new neighbor, and her friendship with Mr. Harrison forms another plot thread. Mr. Harrison serves three purposes in the story. His down-to-earth view of the human condition contrasts with Anne's idealism. As one of the "odd" people of the novel, Mr. Harrison challenges Avonlea's view of propriety by keeping a parrot and washing his dishes only when it rains. Anne's fondness for him, and later for the unconventional Miss Lavendar, reflects Montgomery's impatience with the strict norms of her own village where, as in Avonlea, any unexpected behavior was considered "barely respectable" (*AA*, 4). Finally, Montgomery's favorite theme of reunion is treated comically in Mr. Harrison's reconciliation with his estranged wife, a theme later treated more seriously in the story of Miss Lavendar. Again, an explosion is important to the plot thread: lightning destroys Mr. Harrison's profane parrot and removes the major impediment to his reconciliation with Emily, the zealous housewife and guardian of respectability.

Near the middle of the novel, the focus shifts to Mrs. Charlotte E. Morgan, whose romantic novels have brought her fame and fortune. Anne's delight at the prospect of meeting a distinguished author mixes with uncertainty about her ability to handle the situation. The results are comic: she overprepares for the expected visit (Waterston and Rubio, 1987; *AA*, 279), which leads not only to disappointment because of Mrs. Morgan's initial failure to appear but to another "explosion," as Davy sends a treasured willowware platter crashing down the stairs. When Mrs. Morgan finally appears unexpectedly, Anne is covered with feathers from a bedtick and, through confusion of a freckle potion with red dye, has dyed her nose red. Mrs. Morgan represents the literary success Montgomery hoped to attain, but Anne's problems in dealing with the author's appearance at Green Gables may reflect some of Montgomery's ambiguous feelings about fame and fortune.

In the latter part of the novel, Anne meets Miss Lavendar Lewis and helps to bring about her romantic reunion with a lover absent for 25 years, a plot device that uses the Sleeping Beauty archetype. Miss Lavendar is also "odd" by Avonlea standards, an unmarried woman who refuses to follow the conventional pattern of spinsterhood, who isolates herself from society, and who fills the emptiness of her life by preparing tea for imaginary guests and mothering a "little dream boy" (*AA*, 329). The novel's final "explosion" of sound comes just after Miss Lavendar's wedding when Paul rings the dinner bell and the echoes respond as the princess rides away with her prince (Waterston and Rubio, 1987; *AA*, 281). The romanticism and sentimentality of the Miss Lavendar plot happily are tempered by comic realism. A principal technique of the comedy is bathos; while the fairy-tale romance appeals to Anne's poetic spirit, Marilla and the little maidservant, Charlotta the Fourth, insist on stating it in "prose."

Anne of Avonlea has, then, the conventional "happily ever after" ending, but the romance is Miss Lavendar's rather than Anne's. There are hints that the heroine's friendship with Gilbert will blossom into romance, but the time has not yet come. The Anne-Gilbert relationship is the slightest of the plot threads and the only one in which there is no "explosion," no fireworks at all, although Anne does, in the last chapter, feel her heart flutter strangely in Gilbert's presence and wonders if romance may not unfold quietly and naturally from friendship. Perhaps this thought is related to Montgomery's relationship with the Reverend Ewan Macdonald, to whom she was engaged at the time of the writing of *Anne of Avonlea*. Her journals reveal that she felt no grand passion for Ewan but valued his friendship and was "very fond" of him (*Journals* I, 323). Would this be enough? Is she, through Anne, trying to convince herself that the romance she craves can grow out of simple friendship?

While writing *Anne of Avonlea*, Montgomery experienced bouts of depression. She was confused about her relationship with Ewan and felt her life restricted by her grandmother's demands and the narrowness of village life. She wrote to Ephraim Weber of the "petty spite and meanness" of those who had called themselves her friends (*Weber*, 75), commenting that, "if you have lived all your life in a little village . . . and if you are foolish enough to do something which the others in the village cannot do, especially if that something brings you a small modicum of fame and fortune, a certain class of people will take it as a personal insult to themselves, will belittle you and your accomplishment in every way and will go out of their way to make sure that you are informed of their opinions" (*Weber*, 78–79). A cheerful book was due her young readers, and they were given one, but Avonlea's distrust of those who are different—Paul Irving, Mr. Harrison, and Miss Lavender—reveals some of the author's dissatisfaction with her own environment.

Although still imaginative, impulsive, and inclined toward misadventures, the older Anne has become less a rebellious individualist, more a conformist, and therefore, less interesting. Some of the appealing qualities of the young Anne are transferred to Davy and less successfully to Paul. The sequel is more didactic than its predecessor, with moral comments from Anne, from the minister's wife, and occasionally from the intrusive author. From time to time, the author also tells us directly what a wonderful girl Anne is, an intrusion that rarely occurs in *Anne of Green Gables*. The story of Hester Gray is pure sentimentality, bearing little connection with the rest of the plot other than to introduce another odd isolate from the community. In spite of these weaknesses, however, the novel is appealing in its comic characters and effective dialogue. All sorts of men, women, and children inhabit Avonlea, many made comic by the time-honored device of exaggeration of a single trait. Among those added to the Montgomery comic portrait gallery are the exceedingly pessimistic Miss Eliza Andrews, the henpecked Daniel Blair, the obsessively neat Mrs. Theodore White, and the insatiably curious Davy with his comic repetition of "I want to know." There is also Charlotta the Fourth, with enormous blue bows, wide smiles, and unwavering faith in the superiority of Miss Lavendar, who speaks always in prose and sums up the fairy-tale romance of her employer with, "When all's said and done, Miss Shirley, ma'am, there's many a worse thing than a husband" (*AA*, 346).

Although the point of view is omniscient, with Anne as the principal viewpoint character, the reader does not remain long with any one character. The chief method of characterization and narration is dialogue, with about 75 percent of the text made up of spoken words, a typical percentage for a Montgomery novel.

Writing to Weber of *Anne of Avonlea*, Montgomery hoped this would be her last Anne novel but feared that yet another sequel might be required. Her publishers, she wrote, had wanted the first sequel, "and I'm awfully afraid if the thing takes, they'll want me to write her through college. The idea makes me sick. I feel like the magician in the Eastern story who became the slave of the 'jinn' he had conjured out of a bottle. If I'm to be dragged at Anne's chariot wheels the rest of my life I'll bitterly repent having 'created' her" (*Weber*, 74). Her words proved prophetic for, five years later, Montgomery, to satisfy her publishers and her public, set out to write Anne through college in *Anne of the Island*.

Anne of the Island

Between the publication of *Anne of Avonlea* and the return to the Anne series, Montgomery published four other books. She married Ewan Macdonald, became the mistress of the Presbyterian manse at Leaskdale, Ontario, and gave birth to her first son. When, after seven months of preliminary planning, she began writing *Anne of the Island*, in April 1914, she was pregnant with her second child, deeply distressed by the events of World War I, and doggedly pursuing the duties expected of a minister's wife. In August her second son was born dead. Certainly circumstances were adverse to writing the type of hopeful and instructive book considered appropriate for young readers, but she persevered. In November 1914, 10 days before her fortieth birthday, she wrote in her journal: "I finished 'Anne of Redmond' today. And I am very glad. Never did I write a book under greater stress. All last winter and spring I was physically wretched and all this fall I have been racked with worry over the war and tortured with grief over the loss of my baby. From a literary point of view I don't think much of it. Yet there is some fairly good material in it" (*Journals* II, 156). The publishers saw fit to change the title from *Anne of Redmond* to *Anne of the Island*.

Jon Stott considers the early Anne books more successful than the later ones because in them the heroine is still striving toward goals, and such struggles toward accomplishment are "the stuff of which good stories are made" (Stott, 418). In the third Anne book the 18-year-old protagonist reaches toward three goals: completing a college education, achieving success as a writer, and fulfilling her desire for domestic happiness through marriage. Around her progress toward these three goals the plot is built.

Near the end of *Anne of Avonlea*, Marilla invites the widowed Rachel Lynde to be her companion at Green Gables, releasing Anne to pursue her college studies. Higher education for women was still suspect in Avonlea (and in Cavendish) at the turn of the century, and Anne, the first Avonlea girl to go to college, encounters community skepticism. Rachel Lynde does not approve of "them coeducational places" where students probably do not "ever do much else than flirt."[4] Mrs. Levi Boulter believes Anne is going to college merely "to catch a man" (*AI*, 10), Mrs. Peter Sloane doubts female strength adequate for four years of demanding study, and Mrs. Eben Wright is concerned with the feasibility of financing higher education for a woman (*AI*, 15–16). While at Dalhousie College in 1896, Montgomery had written an essay, published in a local newspaper as "A Girl's Place at Dalhousie College," in which she defended college education not only for professional women but for housewives. At that time only 25 coeds had graduated from Dalhousie since the admission of women in 1881;[5] Anne, like her creator, was a pioneer.

"Kingsport" in Nova Scotia where Anne attends Redmond is, according to Montgomery, "more or less" Halifax, where the author studied at Dalhousie. However, she is careful to add that Anne's experiences are "certainly not a reflection of my own" (*Journals* II, 170). She did enjoy walks through Point Pleasant

Park, overlooking the Halifax harbor and the fortress on George's Island, just as Anne is fond of walking in "the park" and viewing an autumn sunset over "William's Island." For Montgomery old St. Paul's Cemetery in Halifax was as fascinating a place as "St. John's Cemetery" is for Anne. Montgomery read a paper on Ian McLaren for the Philomathic Literary Society; Anne reads one on Tennyson to the Philomathic. Like her heroine, Montgomery was successful academically, particularly in the field of English literature, and, like Anne, experienced homesickness for her island home. Montgomery, however, roomed in Halifax Ladies College and made no close friends, never experiencing anything like the cozy good times Anne had at Patty's Place. Anne spends her Christmas and summer vacations in the loving atmosphere of Green Gables; Montgomery did not return to Cavendish for Christmas break because she felt Grandfather Macneill did not "want to be bothered" with transporting her to and from the train station (*Journals* I, 150). Also, Anne completes four years of study and earns a bachelor of arts degree; Montgomery spent only one year as a special student at Dalhousie.

Montgomery wrote of *Anne of the Island* that there was "less of real life in it than in any of my other books," meaning that fewer incidents from her own life were woven into the plot. All of the story, she says, is "lies and nothing else," except for the afternoon spent by Anne and Priscilla in the old cemetery and for the incident of chloroforming the cat, Rusty, which is modeled on a similar experience of the author and her cousin Frede Campbell (*Journals* II, 170). In real life the cat was successfully destroyed while Anne's Rusty survives, no doubt in deference to the sensibilities of young readers. Although several other of Anne's experiences reflect "more or less" the author's Dalhousie years, the general atmosphere is indeed different.

Another of Anne's goals is to attain success as a writer. She composes a sentimental story, "Averil's Atonement," which she plans to submit to a magazine. Montgomery uses Mr. Harrison's excellent criticism of Anne's story (*AI*, 119–21) to comment on some of her own melodramatic tendencies, which she recognized and, in part, overcame. She followed Mr. Harrison's advice to write of people and places she knew and to "put a little spice of human nature" into her characters, and she generally avoided "high-flown language" except in love scenes, which she seldom handled well. The "flowery descriptions" to which Mr. Harrison objects remained a problem for her, and she was reluctant to "let the sun rise and set in the usual quiet way." It is ironic that, in spite of her recognition of the validity of Mr. Harrison's advice, *Anne of the Island* contains no fewer than six descriptions of sunsets (Gillen, 1975, 175), in which the author displays her love of color, and three contain her favorite color word *purple*. It should be noted, however, that the six descriptions are limited to a total of 218 words. Despite Anne's reluctant revision of "Averil's Atonement," the story is rejected by two periodicals, but, in a comic reversal of Anne's dream of fame, it is published as an advertisement by the Rollings Reliable Baking Powder Company after its editing and clandestine submission by the well-meaning Diana.

Anne has developed as a writer to the extent that she recognizes in her old Story Club efforts a sentimentality so overdone as to make the stories comic. During her last year at Redmond she takes an important step in her writing career when her "garden idyll" is accepted by a periodical. This sketch, written during the period of *Anne of Avonlea*, was composed during her search for a willowware platter to replace the one broken by Davy. The sketch was not felt to be marketable because it did not conform to the usual story pattern preferred by magazine editors. Waterston and Rubio believe it significant that Anne gains literary success after the breaking of a "patterned platter" (Waterston and Rubio, 1987; *AA*, 281). Willingness to depart from the conventional, to break the pattern, is the mark of a true artist.

Montgomery was, however, no pattern breaker in *Anne of the Island*. She focuses primarily on the Anne-Gilbert relationship, which essentially repeats the pattern of popular sentimental fiction that centers around the theme of courtship with marriage as the inevitable happy ending. She was, of course, yielding to the demands of readers who were anxious to see Anne and Gilbert happily united. "I must at least engage Anne for I'll never be given any rest until I do," she wrote in her journal (*Journals* II, 133). If her readers wanted courtship and marriage, she would supply it in abundance, for the book contains not only the happy culmination of Gilbert's pursuit of Anne but five other successful courtships. Among Anne's contemporaries, Philippa Grant is married to her Jonas, Jane Andrews to a Winnipeg millionaire, and Diana to the faithful Fred. Middle-aged romances, of which Montgomery was particularly fond, include Janet Sweet's marriage to John Douglas after a 20-year courtship and Amelia Skinner's "tying up" with the poor but lovable Thomas. In the Janet-John romance the blocking agent is a promise made by John to his supposedly dying mother, a motif repeated throughout Montgomery's fiction.

In these stories of romance Montgomery leavens sentiment, at which she did not excel, with humor, at which she did. Philippa feels unprepared for her role as a minister's wife, particularly fearing that she may be expected "to lead in prayer" (*AI*, 213). The brief story of Jane Andrews's romance is enlivened when Mrs. Harmon Andrews boasts of Jane's "wedding tower" (*AI*, 308) and Rachel Lynde offers straightforward comments on the groom. The marriage of Diana, Anne's loyal friend, to the prosaic Fred is treated respectfully, but the nervous bride's fear that she may faint provokes Anne to threaten to duck her in the rainwater hogshead, and the unromantic Fred ambles into the ceremony with a red face. Anne attempts to advance Janet's romance by urging her to take a firm stand, but then ironically lacks firmness when she practically drags the rejected John back to Janet. Amelia Skinner's ungrammatical account of her alliance with Thomas is humorous in its unlikely candidate for romance, its mispronunciations, and its repetition of the command "Jog along, black mare" (*AI*, 246–49).

Appropriately, Gilbert is featured more prominently in this novel than in the two previous Anne books but is far from omnipresent, appearing or being mentioned in 26 of the 41 chapters. Gilbert is put aside completely for two incidents intended as further steps in Anne's development, the death of Ruby Gillis and Anne's visit to the home of the parents she never knew. The death of the beautiful but worldly Ruby uses obvious pathos and sentimentality but causes Anne to realize her own mortality and to treasure the permanent above the transitory. In her visit to the home of her parents and in their letters, Anne discovers her roots and feels that she is "not an orphan any longer" (*AI*, 195). Also, Gilbert is not mentioned in the chapters concentrating on Janet Sweet, which blend humor and sentiment, and in some of the comic Davy episodes.

The conventional pattern of the Anne-Gilbert plot strews obstacles in the unsmooth path of true love. The chief obstacle is Anne's own reluctance to relinquish her romantic dream of a melancholy, inscrutable, Byronic lover and to recognize her love for her schoolboy friend. Anne believes that she has found her ideal Prince Charming in Royal Gardner, whose very name is princely, deluding herself and her friends through 14 chapters but ultimately discovering that she cannot marry him.

Gilbert misunderstands her relationship to Royal, and Anne misunderstands his attentions to Christine Stuart. Anne's anagnorisis comes on a stormy night, when she believes Gilbert to be dying. The device of recognizing true love when the loved one is dangerously ill is a trite one used by Montgomery in other stories, but it contains a fundamental truth: we often most clearly recognize the value of something when we are about to lose it.

Writing in her journal of this third Anne book, Montgomery acknowledges her principal strength: "Anne is grown-up and can't be made as interesting as when a child. My forte is in writing humor. Only childhood and elderly people can be treated humorously in books. Young women in the bloom of youth should be sacred from humor. It is the time of sentiment and I am not good at depicting sentiment—I can't do it well" (*Journals* II, 133). She liberally interjects into her novel of sentiment the humor of childhood, through a continuation of the escapades and remarks of Davy. She also supplies more mature comic characters, such as Anne's first landlady, who displays an excessive love of embroidered cushions; Mrs. Lilly, a hypochondriac who greets the mention of any ailment with "Ah, I know too well what that is" (*AI*, 209); and Amelia Skinner, who appreciates the "pictureskew" (*AI*, 247). She even breaks her rule of keeping young girls sacred from humor with Priscilla Grant and her excessive indecisiveness.

In the closing paragraph, Gilbert kisses Anne and the two walk together through meadows where blow "winds of hope and memory." Certainly the reader has not been denied a happily-ever-after ending, and Montgomery intended to close Anne's career, hoping her publishers and her readers would now be satisfied. Such was not the case; one year later she began work on a fourth novel about Anne.

Anne's House of Dreams

Montgomery began writing *Anne's House of Dreams* in the summer of 1916 and completed the book within four months. In October 1916 she wrote in her journal, "Today I finished 'Anne's House of Dreams.' I never wrote a book in so short a time and amid so much strain of mind and body. Yet I rather enjoyed writing it and think it isn't too bad a piece of work" (*Journals* II, 193). During the summer and early fall she had been troubled by cystitis, was "rundown" physically (*Journals* II, 146), and continued to agonize over the war news. Moreover, she wrote while caring for a husband afflicted with neuritis as well as for four-year-old Chester and infant Stuart. Bearing three children within four years had taken its physical toll. The demands of Red Cross work, church meetings, and domestic duties were performed during the unusually hot summer of 1916. The idyllic life of Anne in her "house of dreams" seemed far removed from life at the Leaskdale manse, perhaps the reason she "rather enjoyed" this form of escapism as she again made Anne the center of a life quite different from her own.

In *Anne's House of Dreams* the titular heroine exults in natural beauty and in new relationships, but the story focuses primarily on Anne at only four points: her wedding, the death of her first child, her delight in mothering a second, healthy child, and, in the conclusion, her sorrow at the necessity of change as she moves away from her house of dreams. The adult Anne, who has become the village doctor's wife, conforms to social norms. Perhaps because she feels that no great narrative interest can be supplied by Anne's domestic happiness, Montgomery focuses on three other stories: the romantic tale of Captain Jim and his lost Margaret; the fairy-tale romance of Leslie Moore; and the antiromantic story of Cornelia Bryant, an inveterate man hater who unexpectedly decides to enter into the state of matrimony. Anne is present to sympathize, admire, be amused, and sometimes moralize, but these three characters carry the story.

Captain Jim is the first neighbor that Anne and Gilbert meet when they arrive at their new home. Early in the book, he supplies a slight suspense as Anne notices that his eyes seem to hold a "wistful quest in them, as of one seeking something precious and lost."[6] She and Miss Cornelia wonder about his lonely bachelorhood, and the narrator refers cryptically to his possession of "a memory" (*AHD*, 66). The mystery is dispelled when, midway through the book, Captain Jim tells the story of his "lost Margaret" (*AHD*, 129–30). The sentimental story is made appealing by Captain Jim's colloquial narration. Captain Jim is the lighthouse keeper, and the beacon he tends, one of the several light images in the novel, becomes a symbol of the love and kindness that the captain brings to Anne and other inhabitants of Four Winds. The brief account of Captain Jim's death is sentimental—the old man sails away in the dawn's light toward love awaiting him in the life beyond, while leaving behind love in the hearts of his friends—but it repeats the recurring light imagery and seems appropriate to the general tone and atmosphere of the novel.

Captain Jim comments on popular literature, criticizing the weaknesses of fiction that conforms to the dictates of popular taste. Expecting a romantic story to end with a wedding, Captain Jim becomes impatient with the number and length of the complications that postpone the inevitable ending. Of one such story he says, "I'm reading it jest to see how long she can spin it out. It's at the sixty-second chapter now, but the wedding ain't any nearer than when it begun, far's I can see" (*AHD*, 60–61). He also questions the realism of the conventional ending: "When they got married, the book stopped right off, so I reckon their troubles were all over. It's real nice that that's the way in books anyhow, isn't it, even if 'tisn't so anywhere else?" (*AHD*, 119). Montgomery's own tendency to adopt the predictable patterns of sentimental novels is deprecated by Gillian Thomas and T. D. MacLulich. Thomas writes, "The idea that some marriages can be unfulfilled or destructive is scarcely allowed to intrude in Anne's world."[7] MacLulich deplores the fact that, when Montgomery wrote of adults rather than children, "she succumbed to formulas of popular sentimental fiction, and filled her pages with variations on the theme of courtship, using marriage as the happy ending that makes up for any amount of prior suffering."[8]

In *Anne's House of Dreams* the one unhappy marriage, that of Leslie and Dick Moore, is set right when the old device of mistaken identity is brought into play, and Leslie is freed from her bondage for a marriage of true love with Owen Ford. In creating Leslie, Montgomery reworked the familiar fairy tale of "The Goose Girl" so obviously that the beautiful Leslie actually is driving a flock of white geese when first seen by Anne. In Grimm's story the princess is forced to work as a goose girl, has long golden hair that she unlooses when in the meadows, is imprisoned in an iron oven, and is freed to marry the prince when her real identity is discovered. Leslie has unusual beauty and intelligence, possesses long golden hair that "reaches to her feet when she lets it down" (*AHD*, 75), is imprisoned in her union with the supposed Dick, and is freed when the truth is revealed. Also, Leslie reminds Owen of the myth of Danae surrounded by a cloud of gold (*AHD*, 163), another story of imprisonment and release.

The character of Leslie provides the novel's principal story line, beginning with the mystery of Leslie's identity and, later, her unexplained hostility toward Anne. In chapter 11 Miss Cornelia describes Leslie's pathetic situation, and the mystery is replaced by the suspense of the uncertain outcome of "Dick's" operation and of Leslie's relationship with Owen Ford. Her predicament is solved by the use of the device of the double; Mr. Hyde (Dick) becomes Dr. Jekyll (George), who is not married to Leslie at all. The intended surprise of the outcome is legitimate, clues having been planted throughout the story—the supposed Dick's basically pleasant nature, his plumpness, and his being ignored by his dog on returning from his sea voyage.

In telling Leslie's story, Montgomery uses the kind of overblown language that she seemed to feel such a tale demands. Leslie goes on and on about her "twisted heartstrings" (*AHD*, 168), and even Anne seriously advises Leslie against dwelling on thoughts "that only harrow your soul unavailingly" (*AHD*, 136). Owen's proposal, in the garden of the house of dreams, is the zenith, or nadir, of unrealistic, sentimental language, with its talk of roses that "hold all the warmth and soul of the summer come to fruition." Did any real man, however besotted, ever speak as does Owen Ford?

> "The pink roses are love hopeful and expectant—the white roses are love dead or forsaken—but the red roses—ah, Leslie, what are the red roses?"
> "Love triumphant," said Leslie in a low voice. (*AHD*, 230)

"Not low enough," writes Elizabeth Waterston, commenting on the "false strain" in the scene (Waterston, 1975, 18). Regrettably, on this occasion there is no Miss Cornelia nearby to bring us humorously back to the world of reality, as she does in an earlier scene in which Owen sees fit to comment on the "prisoned infinite" calling out to the "kindred infinite." Miss Cornelia advises, "You seem to have a cold in the head. Better rub some tallow on your nose when you go to bed." The reader laughs and blesses Miss Cornelia who personates "the comedy that ever peeps around the corner at the tragedy of life" and in whose presence the "high falutin' language" of sentiment shrinks away (*AHD*, 164).

Waterston and Rubio find it significant that L. M. Montgomery gives the "trapped" Leslie Moore her own initials: "Like Montgomery, Leslie had compromised her own desire, had been tied to her duty to an older maternal figure, and had accepted a husband thrust on her by force of circumstance."[9]

Leslie is a useful foil to Anne: one is embittered and frustrated while the other is happy and fulfilled. She also provides the major suspense in the novel. But it is Miss Cornelia, Montgomery's most successful comic character since the young Anne of Green Gables, who gives the story its liveliness. Miss Cornelia excels in verbal irony ("His father threw a stump at him when he was small. Nice gentle missile, wasn't it?") and in the humor of unexpectedly apt comparisons ("His face just looks like one of those long narrow stones in the graveyard. 'Sacred to the memory' ought to be written on his forehead") (*AHD*, 54, 52). She is alert to others' inconsistencies and laughs at the infidel who hates church but loves to sing, warbling "Safe in the Arms of Jesus" at a funeral (*AHD*, 49). She is less aware of incongruities in herself, deciding against wearing a wedding veil with a navy blue dress because she "doesn't want to be different from other people" when, as the narrator notes, she is "not noticeably like anyone else on the face of the earth" (*AHD*, 227). Her constant belittling of men and Methodists becomes a humorous exaggerated trait, as does her reiterated expression "just like a man." Into the mouth of Miss Cornelia, Montgomery places some of the most appealing of what Mollie Gillen calls her "capsule characterizations" (Gillen, 1975, 175): "He's so slow on the uptake that he stands still for five minutes before it dawns on him that he's stopped" (*AHD*, 54). When the ardent feminist makes her startling announcement that she is to be married in spite of her distrust of men, the reader delights in the unexpectedness of the situation and in Miss Cornelia's defense of her reversal as she vows that the scarcity and inaptitude of hired men "would drive anyone to get married" (*AHD*, 226).

Another welcome comic character is Susan Baker, the devoted domestic assistant at the house of dreams, who arrives during Anne's first pregnancy and becomes a permanent fixture. As outspoken in her admiration of men as Miss Cornelia is in her dislike of them, Susan frequently bemoans her single state. Her favorite phrases are "Susan is at the helm" and "that you may tie to," and she is as adept at unexpected comparisons ("puffing like a hen drawing rails") as is Miss Cornelia (*AHD*, 233).

Now that Anne has found domestic happiness, she still composes, and sometimes sells, "fanciful little sketches" (*AHD*, 16), but she does little writing. The fading of Anne's literary ambition as she adopts the career of wife and mother may reflect Montgomery's own ambiguity about the proper sphere for a woman, or she may simply be conforming to the expectations of her reading public. Male characters, Paul Irving and Owen Ford, are permitted careers as writers, but Anne subjugates her literary talents to a conventional domestic role.

Although Anne's experiences in her house of dreams generally are quite different from Montgomery's in the Leaskdale manse, the author does draw on some elements from her own experience. Two china dogs, Gog and Magog, sit on either side of the fireplace in Anne's home, having been sent as a wedding gift by Miss Patty, the knitting globe-trotter of *Anne of the Island*. On her honeymoon trip to England and Scotland, Montgomery purchased a pair of china dogs more than a hundred years old, named them Gog and Magog for the followers of Satan who warred against God, and proudly installed them in her new house, no doubt aware of the irony of giving the inhabitants of a minister's residence such names (Gillen, 1975, 98). These household gods are the only relic in her books of her travel abroad.

The author also drew from her own experience to depict Anne's grief at the death of an infant. When little Hugh Alexander Macdonald was born dead, his mother grieved that a long-awaited child should die while many unwanted children lived. She bitterly questioned such proffered platitudes as "The baby is better off" and "It is God's will" and found no comfort in the thought of reunion with her child in the afterlife, for there he might be no longer a baby. The subsequent birth of Stuart was a time of rejoicing, but she rejected any suggestion that this child could replace little Hugh (*Journals* II, 151, 153, 173). These reactions recorded in her journals are transferred practically verbatim to Anne's reactions to the death of little Joyce.

According to one journal entry, in the creation of the Four Winds harbor, site of the house of dreams, Montgomery had in mind the New London harbor, although some alterations were made in the geography (*Journals* II, 222). This book, more than any other, reflects the author's lifelong love of the sea. Some of the stories told by Captain Jim came from anecdotes related by her grandfather. Another scrap of real-life experience is Miss Cornelia's description of those whom she finds congenial as members of "the race that knows Joseph" (*AHD*, 42). The phrase, adapted from Exodus 1:8, was coined by Montgomery's favorite cousin, Frederica ("Frede") Campbell.

In *Anne's House of Dreams* Montgomery's descriptions of the natural environment effectively merge characters and events with their surroundings. Elizabeth Epperly believes that the elements that "stifled" Montgomery's poetry, such as the abundance of color and jewel imagery, add life to the prose and produce an appropriate atmosphere.[10] In Anne's first glimpse of Four Winds, she sees a sea "like a great shining mirror of rose and silver," a little fishing village "like a great opal," and the sky above "like a jeweled cup" (*AHD*, 25). These and numerous other images of color and brightness throughout the novel manifest the vivid personality of Anne and her joyous response to her new life. But all is not brightness, for, in the same description, we read of the "dim sails" that drift along the "darkening, fir-clad harbor shore" (*AHD*, 25). Anne's life will have its shadows—the death of her firstborn, her involvement with the unhappy Leslie, and the death of her good friend Captain Jim.

Description often is used to enhance characterization. Leslie's house is gray and gloomy, but when the beam from the lighthouse touches its windows, they glow out of "its quiet and grayness like the throbbing blood-red thoughts of a vivid soul imprisoned in the dull husk of environment" (*AHD*, 57). The beam from Captain Jim's lighthouse brings, like its guardian, the light of love, kindness, and wisdom. A hearth fire, mentioned 16 times in the novel, is symbolic of the love that warms the house of dreams. The vivid green of Miss Cornelia's house is as startling as is the house's owner, but there is a "certain bareness" about the whole establishment, "so starkly neat" (*AHD*, 26), reflecting Miss Cornelia's adherence to the Puritan work ethic and the barrenness of her life.

Through extensive use of pathetic fallacy, the author makes the natural world reflect the character's moods (Epperly, 41). On an evening of gray fog when the sea "sobbed and shuddered" (*AHD*, 87), Anne observes Leslie's agonized weeping over the darkness of her existence. Anne experiences the happiness of giving birth to a child at dawn "when the rising sun rent apart the mists hanging over the sandbar and made rainbows of them" (*AHD*, 123), but at sunset, heartbreak comes. Another child is born when "a windy golden sunrise" billows over the gulf in "waves of light" (*AHD*, 204). On the occasion of Owen's confession to Anne of his seemingly hopeless love of Leslie, the evening wind in the poplars sounds "like some sad, weird, old rune," but a single young aspen, "slender" and "shapely" like Leslie, stands against the colorful western sky as a symbol of hope (*AHD*, 164;

Epperly, 41). Gilbert makes his decision concerning the operation that may restore Dick's mental powers during the ugliness of early spring when the harbor ice is "rotten-black" (*AHD*, 178), and for a time Leslie's future appears cold and dark. Spring, however, brings laughter to the waves, a gleam to the red harbor road, bright flames from the burning of sandhill grass, and joy to Leslie. The benevolent lighthouse beacon still shines after the death of Captain Jim; his influence is still felt. Associating the light with her happiness in the house of dreams, Anne does not want to move away from its gleam but is assured by Gilbert that the beacon may be seen from the attic window of her new home. As Anne says goodbye to the house of dreams, the "lighthouse star" (*AHD*, 245) throws its beam toward the north as a sign of further happiness in the new home at Ingleside.

The three Anne sequels appearing before 1918 were written by Montgomery to please her public rather than herself. They contain elements of the sentimental novel, such as courtships culminating in happy marriages, promises made to the dying, reunions of estranged lovers, and pathetic death scenes. Montgomery handled the patterns distinctively by liberally inserting her characteristic humor. Because the comic tends to overshadow the sentimental, these novels continue to entertain long after other popular novels of the period have been forgotten. Montgomery was to continue the saga of Anne, not by her own choice but because she had created a heroine that her readers would not willingly let die.

4

More about Anne: 1919–1939

Montgomery had been unexpectedly pleased with the outcome of *Anne's House of Dreams*, labeling it "the best I have ever written not even excepting *Green Gables* or my own favorite 'The Story Girl'" (*Journals* II, 222). With this feeling of accomplishment, she was probably less reluctant than usual to return to Anne's world and began plans for *Rainbow Valley* just three months after completing the story of the house of dreams. Still she cited the demands of her publishers and her public as justification for continuing to write in a style she was "tired" of and had "outgrown" (*Journals* II, 278).

Rainbow Valley

According to the journals, *Rainbow Valley* was completed on Christmas Eve 1918. The idea of pushing Anne into the background, successful in the previous book, is carried even further. This novel focuses on Anne's children and their young friends.

In the book, described by Rosamond Bailey as "a novel without a protagonist,"[1] Anne has six children, ranging in age from 6 to 13. Walter's love of beauty, fanciful dreams, and bookish talk recall the young Anne, but Montgomery was never as interested in children of happy, two-parent homes as she was in the orphans and half-orphans who abound in her books. Here the principal characters are not Anne and her offspring but the four motherless Meredith children of the Presbyterian manse and their new companion, the orphan Mary Vance.

The manse children are the major source of the book's humor and its pathos. The incidents in which the children's good intentions bring disastrous results are humorous but tinged with the pathetic when adults inflict misery on innocent, well-intentioned children. After a loyal churchman gives his prayer meeting testimony with "fearful groans," Jerry asks, "Do you feel any better now?"[2]; his genuine sympathy is misinterpreted as impertinence. Knowing that their untidy home is the target of community criticism, Faith and Una clean house on Sunday, mistakenly believing the day to be Saturday, and Faith's explanation in church, an act of courage and good intent, ironically makes matters worse since it is seen as bold and defiant. Faith compassionately gives her own shoes and stockings to the barefooted child of a fisherman and subsequently scandalizes members of her Presbyterian congregation by appearing in church without stockings and showing "two good inches of bare white leg" (*RV*, 262). Again attempting to set matters straight, Faith writes a letter to the local paper that is a masterpiece of honesty and unwitting criticism, which scandalizes her neighbors.

Society's expectations of a minister's family were well known to Montgomery. In previous books she documented the intolerance and petty gossip that she felt characterized village life, but her distaste for social hypocrisy is particularly evident here. Even Miss Cordelia, ever mindful of what the Methodists might say, sees only the improprieties of the manse children until Anne helps her to recognize their virtues.

Humorous incidents involving the manse children descend to the level of farce more often than is true in previous books of the series. Faith and Walter ride pigs down the main street; the overbearing Mrs. Alec Davis stumbles over Carl's pet toad and staggers across the room; Faith quietly watches the coattails of the sanctimonious Reverend Perry catch on fire; and Carl throws an eel into the buggy of Mrs. Carr, causing that estimable lady to jump over the wheels. Young readers delight in such comedy, particularly when adults are the victims, but adults prefer the verbal comedy supplied by Miss Cornelia and

Susan Baker and by Faith's oral and written attempts to exonerate the family.

The motherless condition of the manse children sometimes is belabored to the point of sentimentality. When Una reads her mother's recipes to assuage her hunger for appetizing food and talks lovingly to her mother's wedding dress, the reader feels the author, too obviously, tugging at the heartstrings and is anxious to leave the saccharine pathos of Una and return to the escapades of the irrepressible Faith.

Another neglected child is Mary Vance, the runaway orphan befriended by the manse children. Mary is about the age Anne was when she came to Green Gables and, like Anne, is plucky and voluble. But Mary is a new breed of orphan, boastful, condescending, and, although basically kind, tactless and insensitive. Mary has been not only neglected but actually abused by the guardian who took a "home child" to be an unpaid household slave. Mary, who boasts of her "lickings" as she boasts of everything else, is a realistic psychological study, in which the author shows admirable restraint. Readers are allowed to draw their own conclusions about the causes of Mary's braggadocio. Her lecturing, condescension, and delight in telling the manse children unpleasant news are not endearing traits, but she is a more realistic character than the gentle, faultless Una. She adds spice to the story as she pushes her way through an unfriendly world, boasting of beatings when she lacks any other claim to superiority and in church, wearing shabby, borrowed clothes, lifting her strong voice to carol "His blood can make the *violets* clean" (*RV*, 62). As Rosamond Bailey notes, Mary adds an element of conflict to the harmonious relationship of the Blythes and Merediths. Also, since she is the "self-appointed critic" and reporter of community disapproval, she serves as catalyst for several of the episodes in which the Meredith children seek to improve their reputations (Bailey, 9).

Romantic interest is supplied by the minister's courtship of Rosemary West, who the minister recognizes would fill a vacuum not only in his own life but in the lives of his motherless offspring. The impediment to the marriage of John and Rosemary is a promise made by the latter to her sister Ellen that she would never marry and leave Ellen alone. This type of complication was used in *Anne of the Island* and appears in several of the author's short stories. It is a motif common to the many folk stories in which a promise is made without due consideration of the possible outcome and is sometimes described as the motif of "the damsel's rash promise," the promiser being usually, but not always, a female. Rosemary's release comes through her sister's own desire to marry the man from whom she was estranged 20 years ago, another favorite situation with Montgomery.

As Montgomery continued her writing career, she became repetitious. Jon C. Stott comments, "Characters and actions become predictable; it is as if the author has established a formula and has merely changed details" (Stott, 421). Once again a "rash promise" forms a temporary obstacle to romance and, again, a middle-aged couple is reconciled after years of estrangement. Her most successful formula was the conquering of unsympathetic adults by an appealing child, as Anne melted the armor of Marilla, Rachel Lynde, and Miss Josephine Barry. Following that pattern, the author here has Faith Meredith vanquish the irascible Norman Douglas. Indeed, Faith's outburst of temper toward Douglas is strongly reminiscent of Anne's toward Mrs. Lynde and just as satisfying.

Montgomery must plead guilty to charges of repetition of formulas and occasional sentimentality, but she continues to portray convincingly the feelings of children. Una's fear that a stepmother will model her behavior on that of the cruel stepmothers of fairy tales, Faith's grief over the sacrifice to the cooking pot of her pet rooster, Carl's fear of ghostly creatures during his lonely vigil in the graveyard, and Faith's resentment of Norman Douglas's contemptuous remarks all strike responsive chords in the heart of any child or any adult who remembers the woes of childhood.

The author transferred some of her own experiences to the lives of her young characters. The creeping, white shape that terrifies the manse children recalls the fright of young Maud and her playmates at a similar apparition. Maud's ghost proved to be Grandmother Macneill carrying a white tablecloth on her back while stooping in search of a dropped knitting needle (*Alpine Path*, 31-33); a neighbor frightens the manse children by similar behavior. Walter Blythe, having inherited his mother's fondness for naming things, calls a slender birch tree "White Lady" and a spruce and maple growing close together "Tree Lovers"; Maud had given the same names to trees on her grandparents' Cavendish farm (*Alpine Path*, 33). While a student at Prince of Wales College, Montgomery had coined the term "ditto" for the boiled mutton that was the constant boardinghouse fare (*Journals* I, 103) and uses the label for the manse children's description of Aunt Martha's ever-present cold, greasy mutton. Her son Chester provided material for the incident in which Mary Vance pursues the vain little Rilla Blythe with a dried codfish; Chester gave chase to his young cousin Amy Campbell in like fashion (*Journals* II, 399). During the spring of 1916, Montgomery's journals report three-year-old Chester's fondness for "that absurd old song 'Polly Wolly Doodle'" (*Journals* II, 179). His frequent and lusty rendition of the ditty undoubtedly was the genesis of the manse children's selection of "Polly Wolly Doodle" as the rousing finale for their concert in the Methodist graveyard.

The first four books of the Anne series concern themselves with Anne's immediate environment and scarcely hint at the world beyond Avonlea, Kingsport, or Four Winds. *Rainbow Valley* suggests that a coming world conflict will profoundly affect Anne's little island world. Ellen Douglas insists that danger is embodied in the Kaiser of Germany. Early in the book, Walter speaks prophetically of the future arrival in Rainbow Valley of the Pied Piper, who will pipe wild music that the boys will follows while the girls stay and wait at home. In the final chapter, Walter repeats his prophecy with more urgency: "The Piper is coming nearer. . . . He pipes—he pipes—and we must follow—Jem and Carl and Jerry and I—round and round the world" (*RV*, 340). Montgomery's next book was to concentrate on the piper's call and the devastating effects of war on the children's "fairy realm" (*RV*, 21) of Rainbow Valley.

Rilla of Ingleside

Just three months after the completion of *Rainbow Valley*, Montgomery began to write the book that she intended to be the last of the Anne series. Anne, she wrote, was the inhabitant of a happy world, "the green untroubled pastures and still waters of the world before the war," and there she should remain (*Journals* II, 309). But World War I had been one of the most traumatic experiences of the author's life, and a war novel she must write. In *Rilla of Ingleside*, Anne is in the background, the courageous, suffering mother of sons at the front, and the spotlight is on Anne's youngest daughter, who grows from frivolous girlhood to staunch womanhood during the four troubled years of the war.

The world conflict had ended when the book was initiated, but new troubles beset the author's life. For months she grieved over the death, in January 1919, of Frederica Campbell Mac-Farlane, her first cousin and "kindred spirit," the one friend whom she felt she could completely trust (*Journals* II, 295). During the summer, her husband's bouts of depression were diagnosed as recurrent constitutional melancholia. She began another lawsuit against L. C. Page, this time for the company's unauthorized publication of *Further Chronicles of Avonlea*. To complete a book during a period of such difficulties was an amazing accomplishment, but a great deal of the material was already written. In her journals she had recorded her reactions to the events of World War I, and she used these comments extensively, transferring them, often practically verbatim, to her characters. For example, on 7 December 1914, she wrote in her journal,

> The war is at least extending my knowledge of geography. Six months ago I did not know there was such a place as Lodz. Had I heard it mentioned I would have known nothing about it and cared as little. Today the news that the Germans have captured it in their second drive for Warsaw made my heart sink in my boots. I know all about it now—its size, its standing, its military significance (*Journals* II, 157).

In *Rilla of Ingleside*, Gertrude Oliver, the local schoolteacher who boards with the Ingleside family, comments,

> This war is at least extending my knowledge of geography. Schoolma'am though I am, three months ago I didn't know

there was such a place in the world as Lodz. Had I heard it
mentioned I would have known nothing about it and cared as
little. I know all about it now—its size, its standing, its military significance. Yesterday the news that the Germans have
captured it in their second rush to Warsaw made my heart
sink into my boots.[3]

This example is only one of numerous instances in which Montgomery places passages from her journals into the mouths of
various characters—Gertrude, Anne, Rilla, Walter, Susan
Baker, and the Reverend John Meredith.

The novel begins in June 1914 when the assassination of the
Archduke Ferdinand is reported, along with items of local interest, in the Glen *Notes*. It ends in the spring of 1919 with the
homecoming of Jem Blythe and Kenneth Ford, representatives
of some 540,000 Canadian soldiers who returned from the conflict in which about 60,000 of their countrymen died. Irony is
abundant and perhaps a bit too pointed in the early chapters.
Susan Baker ignores the "immaterial" news of the assassination
in Sarajevo and seeks "something really vital" in the local newspaper (*RI*, 2). Of the same report, Miss Cornelia asks, "What
does it matter to us?" (*RI*, 14). Rilla finds the events of her life
abominably dull and wishes "something dramatic would happen" (*RI*, 20). She has no real problems except the fear that no
one will ask her to dance at her first grown-up party.

The Ingleside family and their neighbors anxiously await
newspaper reports of war news and comment in detail on its
major events. In fact, so thoroughly is historical information
given that at times the novel reads like a textbook on the military campaigns of World War I. To relieve the textbook atmosphere, the author allows many sober events to be seen from the
viewpoint of Susan Baker, the Ingleside housekeeper. In the
early days of the war Susan makes up her mind to be a heroine,
announcing this decision while incongruously clad in a gray
flannel nightgown and wearing a strip of red wool around her
head "as a charm against neuralgia" (*RI*, 79). The self-pro-
claimed heroine sees it as her duty to "grapple" with the tasks at
hand, cutting potato sets, cooking meals, and weeding the onion
patch for "king and country" (*RI*, 231). In her dual concern for

events abroad and immediate household duties, she yokes an unsuccessful batch of bread with the fall of Warsaw. Previously interested only in local gossip, Susan relentlessly follows the news of every campaign, puzzling over, and often mispronouncing, foreign names. She sees Constantine of Greece as "a miserable creature ... under his wife's thumb" (*RI*, 192), and, from the kitchen window nearest the United States, apostrophizes Woodrow Wilson with "Peace is not made with ink, Woodrow, and that you may tie to" (*RI*, 205). Her incorrigible optimism exults in every victory and belittles every defeat as having "no military significance," a phrase acquired from her recent reading about foreign affairs. A comic foil for Susan is supplied by Cousin Sophia Crawford; the pessimistic comments of Cousin Sophia always receive a swift rebuttal from the optimistic Susan. In one farcical episode Susan definitely refuses her first and only proposal of marriage, which comes from a local pacifist. She pursues the unlucky suitor with an iron pot filled with boiling dye. Susan's antics leaven with comedy the recital of war events as well as the sentimentality that threatens to overwhelm this story of patriotic self-sacrifice.

Montgomery presents an account of World War I on all fronts, but Canadian participation in the war receives, not surprisingly, the strongest emphasis. Her journals record that a letter from her publishers complained that the book was too "gloomy" and implied that she gave insufficient attention to the role of the United States in the war. "I wrote of Canada at war," wrote Montgomery, "not the U.S." (*Journals* II, 404). The achievements of the Canadian troops are documented on the pages of *Rilla*, achievements that gave just cause for Canadian pride.

When England declared war, in August 1914, Canada was preparing to celebrate 100 years of peace and had only a small militia. The dominion was officially required to support the British Empire, but the unofficial reaction, at least of Canadians of British descent, was enthusiastic. In September 1914, some 30,000 volunteers of the first Canadian division were brought together at Valcartier in Quebec and sailed for England, where they underwent training on Salisbury Plain. In the fictional account, Jem Blythe, Jerry Meredith, and Gertrude Oliver's fiancé, Robert Grant, are a part of this group, which reached the trenches of France in February 1915. Jem writes home of the cold, the rats, and, to Susan's horror, the "cooties" (*RI*, 134).

In the spring of 1915, the Canadian division began its defense of the Ypres (pronounced by Susan "Ypriz") (*RI*, 129), where they showed their mettle during the first use of poison gas by the Germans. Rilla's second brother, Walter, joins the second Canadian division, as does her friend Kenneth Ford. The Canadian army corps eventually grew to four separately maintained divisions, made up largely of volunteers. In the Battle of the Somme the Canadians distinguished themselves at Courcelette, where Montgomery's half brother Carl was wounded and where the fictional Walter Blythe goes "over the top" (*RI*, 256). The most notable achievement of the Canadian forces was their capture of Vimy Ridge, now the site of a Canadian War Memorial. In the novel, Jerry Meredith is wounded at Vimy Ridge, and a few months later Mary Vance's fiancé loses his leg at the Canadian capture of Hill 70 outside Lens. The Canadians, with other allies, were put on the defensive during the spring of 1918 when Jem Blythe is reported wounded and missing. But in August at the Battle of Amiens—where Carl Meredith is presumably wounded—the tide turns. Canadians fought valiantly at Cambrai and at Valenciennes and made their last successful offensive with the capture of Mons, just a few hours before the signing of the armistice. Canada had no air force, but thousands of Canadians, including Shirley Blythe, joined the Royal Flying Corps. Its outstanding achievements in World War I brought Canada new international recognition.

While soldiers fought in the trenches, patriots on the home front, represented by the Ingleside family, supported their effort by knitting socks, raising funds for the Red Cross, making "vermin shirts," economizing in accordance with the "save and serve" slogan, buying victory bonds, and plowing up their lawns to plant food crops. The Ingleside family supports the union government and its conscription act, as did Montgomery and most English-speaking Canadians. The village of Glen St. Mary, in fact, has only one inhabitant with antiwar sentiments. Montgomery ignores the anti-British feeling and the opposition to conscription of many French-Canadians. Indeed, in her novels she tends to relegate the French to roles of servants with comic accents. Although a thoughtful and well-read woman, she was a product of her ethnic background, including its prejudices.

One character—Gertrude Oliver—is involved in war events through her prophetic dreams. Montgomery drew on her abiding interest in dreams for material and wrote to George MacMillan of her series of strange dreams during the war, every one of which she insisted had "come true" (*MacMillan*, 103). Gertrude has three prophetic dreams, in chapters 3, 19, and 30, and each contains accurate predictions. With her tendency toward bitterness and her religious doubts, as well as her prophetic dreams, Gertrude is probably the character with whom Montgomery most strongly identified.

Important as the progress of the war is to the novel, however, the major plot line is not built around the war itself but around the development of Rilla. Montgomery wrote to MacMillan that this book was more a "girl's story" than the previous two had been (*MacMillan*, 103). Rilla is a convincing adolescent in whom teenagers should be able to recognize some of their own traits and concerns. At the beginning of the book she is almost 15, with her interests confined to parties and good times, to clothes and appearance, and to a desire for popularity. In typical adolescent fashion, she finds life at home rather dull, longs for more excitement, and is in conflict with her mother on the subject of suitable clothes. Minor problems loom large in her adolescent mind as she feels she will "die of mortification" if not asked to dance at the lighthouse party (*RI*, 23) and is embarrassed by her slight lisp to the point of wishing to "throw herself headlong down the lighthouse rock" (*RI*, 39). When mistakenly left behind by the Ingleside group and forced to walk home, she weeps with the conviction that no one cares about her. During the following four years, she becomes less self-centered, conscientiously caring for an abandoned "war baby" and dutifully performing uncongenial tasks such as knitting, sewing, cooking, and child care. When the news of Walter's enlistment comes during a benefit concert for the Junior Red Cross, she places public duty before private feelings and fulfills her responsibilities. The unkind remarks of the once-admired Irene Howard no longer have power to hurt her. She swallows her pride and asks

Irene's help in the concert, and she recites for a good cause in spite of her occasional lisp, which no longer seems humiliating. When she carelessly wears unmatched shoes to a meeting with Irene, she is embarrassed but not devastated and is able to laugh at herself. An expensive and unsuitable green velvet hat, bought by Rilla early in the war and worn relentlessly for four seasons, becomes a symbol of the heroine's frivolity being replaced by determination and self-sacrifice.

Although the novel's point of view is omniscient, Rilla is the principal viewpoint character, and the reader is brought even closer to her through frequent use of the first-person point of view. About one-fifth of the novel is made up of passages from Rilla's diary. Montgomery uses the diary technique of narration again in the books of the *Emily* trilogy.

A love interest must be present to meet the demands of popular fiction, and Rilla awaits the return of Kenneth Ford for whom she has promised to save her kisses. The romance theme, however, is subjugated to the story of Rilla's development and is not sentimentalized. Rilla's meeting with Ken before his departure for overseas duty, potentially a sentimental love scene, is treated humorously, since Rilla has no time for romantic conversation due to the demands of her crying war baby. Also, Susan appears and, ironically determined to help Rilla entertain, recounts embarrassing stories of the heroine's childhood. When Ken returns from war, we are again spared a sentimental love scene as he simply asks, "Is it Rilla-my-Rilla?" and Rilla answers with the book's final lisping word "Yeth" (*RI*, 370).

After Rilla, the character receiving greatest attention is Walter, whose dilemma provides dramatic conflict. A lover of beauty who is repelled by ugliness and pain, Walter is torn between his sense of duty and the repugnance he feels toward bloodshed. His decision to become a soldier is belated and difficult. Both blessed and cursed by the inheritance of his mother's powerful imagination, Walter finds imagined warfare more frightening than the reality and, convinced of the rightness of his decision, becomes a heroic soldier. Helen Porter cites Walter's death as one of several examples of the fact that even death in Montgomery's novels is a part of the author's "fair world" since it comes at the "right time."[4] Walter's last letter shows him to be ready for death, and he continues to live and to inspire his countrymen through his war poem "The Piper." Although this poem and its author are fictitious, it was indeed a Canadian, John McCrae, who wrote the most popular poem of the World War, "In Flanders Fields." When reciting at recruiting meetings, Montgomery always gave as an encore "In Flanders Fields" by the Canadian soldier who, like Walter, died in France (*MacMillan*, 81), and McCrae doubtless contributed to the portrait of Walter. It was not until 21 years later that Montgomery wrote a poem entitled "The Piper" in response to readers' inquiries about Walter's poem. Published in the Canadian magazine *Saturday Night* in 1942, it was her final poem.[5]

Another appealing plot thread is found in the story of the faithful dog Monday, who waits for four years at the train station for his master's return. With her Scottish background, Montgomery doubtless knew the story of Greyfriars Bobby, a tale of canine devotion exhibited by a long vigil. Bobby, an Edinburgh hero, maintained a 14-year watch by the grave of his master in Greyfriars churchyard and, like Monday, resisted all enticements to leave his post. Perhaps she was also influenced by the popularity of the dog stories of Marshall Saunders, in particular *Beautiful Joe*, which had become an international best seller in 1894 and was followed by other novels featuring admirable dogs. Saunders and Montgomery were friends, although the latter secretly found her fellow writer "clever but a bit of a bore" (*Journals* II, 348).

Familiar Montgomery patterns recur in *Rilla*. Again an attractive child wins the heart of a formidable adult as little Jims finds favor with and becomes the heir of a tyrannical elderly woman. Mary Vance saves the life of Jims who suffers with croup, as Anne saved Minnie Mae Barry years before. The use of a promise as a blocking agent to romance appears again as Miranda Pryor refuses to elope with her suitor because of a promise made to her dying mother.

To date, commentary on *Rilla of Ingleside* has focused on the less appealing portrayal of the older Anne, a valid criticism, although here Anne is not intended to be a major character. Fee and Cawker claim that *Rilla* "degenerates into a chauvinistic tract for Canadian support of Great Britain in World War I."[6]

There is some truth in this charge, but *Rilla* is an important book, unique in its vivid fictional treatment of Canada's involvement, both at home and abroad, in the Great War and a convincing portrayal of a girl's emergence from adolescence to maturity.

Montgomery was determined that *Rilla* was to be the last novel about Anne and her family. "I am done with Anne forever," she wrote in her journal. "I swear it as a dark and deadly vow" (*Journals* II, 390). She was true to the vow for 16 years. In 1936, she "very unwillingly" complied with her publishers' request (*MacMillan*, 177) and returned to the world of Anne with *Anne of Windy Poplars*.

Anne of Windy Poplars

In the interim between the writing of *Rilla of Ingleside* and *Anne of Windy Poplars*, Montgomery published eight additional novels; had moved with her family to Norval, Ontario, where she lived for nine years; and, after Ewan's retirement, settled near Toronto, where *Windy Poplars* was completed. Writing to George MacMillan of her response to the request for still another Anne book, she commented, "At first I thought I could never 'get back' into that series. It seemed to belong to another world. But after the plunge I began to find it possible—nay to enjoy it—as if I really had found my way back to those golden years before the world went mad" (*MacMillan*, 177). Written in five months, the book goes back in time to record the life of Anne during the three years between the events of *Anne of the Island* and of *Anne's House of Dreams*. The epistolary method of narration is used in about one-third of the book as Anne, a high school teacher in Summerside, Prince Edward Island, writes to Gilbert in medical school. Montgomery had considerable talent as a letter writer, a gift she here assigns to her heroine. This first-person device brings us close to Anne, who is a more mature version of the Green Gables child with her love of trees, winds, and the sea, her delight in words, and even her propensity for giving names to features of her environment. Realizing that she did not express romantic love well, Montgomery indicates the omission of passages in the letters where Anne presumably gives free rein to words of endearment.

The book was described by the author as "a series of disconnected stories strung together on the thread of Anne's personality" (*MacMillan*, 195), but there is a unifying element. Each of the three sections, marking the three years at Summerside, centers around a major success for Anne as social manager. The first section describes her defeat of the hostile Pringle clan, the second her role in the transformation of the embittered Katherine Brooke, and the third the restoration of Little Elizabeth to her father. Other stories of village life fill out the novel, nine of these being self-contained episodes that could stand alone as short stories but all featuring Anne and her attempts to bring happiness to others.

Anne's irresistible charm and her concern for others enable her to prevent a sulky man from spoiling his daughter's marital prospects, to reunite a nephew with his uncle, and to start a talented young actress on the road to fame. She also changes the lifestyle of an unhappy spinster, conquers the prejudice of an influential family, reconciles estranged lovers, and unites a lonely child with her father. A wealth of unions and reunions is a familiar component of sentimental novels and modern soap operas. Anne's role of "social engineer," a concession to popular taste, makes her a less interesting heroine than the rebellious and imaginative child who transformed Green Gables simply, and innocently, through the power of her personality (Thomas, 1975, 40). Gillian Thomas writes, "If 'serious' literature tends to explore individual consciousness and awareness, then popular literature tends more frequently to celebrate social bonding" (Thomas, 1975, 40). Anne is certainly hard at work at this "social bonding," but the author does permit her two failures to avoid portraying her as a superhuman deus ex machina. Her attempt to save Hazel Marr from an unfortunate marriage backfires, since Hazel does not want to be saved, and her management of the brattish Raymond twins is not an unqualified success. Generally, however, she is so adept in manipulating the lives of others that Rebecca Dew comments, "Well, Miss Shirley, I hope you'll never try to induce me to turn Mohammedan . . . because you'd likely succeed."[7]

That *Anne of Windy Poplars* is repetitious of earlier books cannot be denied. The reunion of lovers estranged by a quarrel (Nora and Jim), the yearning of a sensitive child for love and understanding (Little Elizabeth), and the crusty character who turns out to be less fearsome than anticipated (Franklin West-cott) are situations that have appeared all too frequently in earlier books and contribute to what Elizabeth Waterston has called a "warmed over flavour" (Waterston, 1975, 22). However, Montgomery also repeats what she does best, and this book perhaps has the author's greatest collection of comic characters. Rebecca Dew ironically thinks she bosses the widows, but the reader knows that they diplomatically control the unsuspecting Rebecca. Rebecca is given her comic catch phrase, "This is the last straw." Her constant verbal abuse of the cat, Dusty Miller, changing to threats to leave when he supposedly is given away, provides an appealing comic reversal. The tactless Aunt Mouser recalls all unhappy events of the past that might happen again, introducing her fears of impending disaster with "All I hope is. . . . " Miss Ernestine Bugle, akin to Mrs. Malaprop, is "afraid" of everything—that the new minister's legs indicate a potential dancer, that a neighbor's illness may turn out to be an "alibi," and that she will get her feet wet and catch "ammonia" (*AWP*, 190–95). Mrs. Adoniram Gibson inconsequently adds to each of her remarks on acquaintances the mention of the maiden name of the subject's mother—"I never liked Jim Gregor. His mother was a Tarbush"; "Jane was a good dressmaker. Her mother was a Smiley" (*AWP*, 99, 101). Most readers probably could spare some of Little Elizabeth's dreams of Tomorrow, where her father awaits her, or the unlikely coincidence in which a young amateur photographer—an orphan, of course—supplies a bereaved father with a picture of the deceased child only to discover that the lonely man is the orphan's long-lost uncle. However, the comic characters, including several not mentioned above, are Montgomery at her best.

In a letter to MacMillan, Montgomery wrote that her publishers questioned the inclusion of Anne's walk through the graveyard and her visit to Tomgallon House and felt that these episodes were "too gruesome" (*MacMillan*, 180). The graveyard incident is a collection of vignettes of village life told to Anne by

Miss Valentine Courtaloe and more comic than "gruesome." The Tomgallon incident is an interesting venture into the realm of the Gothic. On an appropriately dark and stormy evening, Anne visits Miss Minerva, "the last of the Tomgallons," who lives alone in a huge, stately house filled with memories of deceased Tomgallons, many of whom died violent deaths. Miss Minerva is convinced that the family is "under a curse" (AWP, 265), and village gossip recalls a story, suggestive of Hawthorne, of the blight placed on Tomgallon House by an angry carpenter. Even this episode, however, is more humorous than gruesome; in fact, it parodies the typical Gothic tale. Miss Minerva is another comic character who takes pride in an abundance of family disasters and couples every commonplace remark with a recollection of family tragedy. For example, she compliments Anne's hair, adding that an unfortunate aunt set fire to her red hair with a candle. After inviting Anne to take a comfortable chair, she supplies the information that her sister had a fatal stroke while sitting there. More chuckles than shivers are provoked by both the graveyard incident and the story of the curse of the Tomgallons.

In 1937, *Reader's Digest* paid Montgomery $3 for permission to quote one sentence from *Anne of Windy Poplars.* "I was just moonlighted into thinking I loved him" (AWP, 201) brought, the author commented, "the highest price I was ever paid for a single line in my life!" (Gillen, 1975, 179).

In 1939, Montgomery signed a contract with R.K.O. for the screen rights to the book, finding this "pleasantly exciting" but puzzling over how a film could be made from the loosely organized plot. Her prediction that the film writers would "inject a good deal of their own invention" (*MacMillan*, 180) proved apt. The 1940 screen production, starring Anne Shirley, retains, with liberal alterations, the Pringle feud, the mellowing of Katherine, and the wistful, psychologically abused Elizabeth. New characters are invented to provide an appropriate role for Slim Summerville, who plays a comic school janitor, and for Henry Travers, cast as a retired seaman who is simpleminded but lovable. Not surprisingly, the love interest is strengthened, and Gilbert, played by Patrick Knowles, makes frequent visits to Pringleton. Melodramatic incidents are added: Katherine is rescued by her admirer from the blazing Pringle mansion, and Anne pursues Matey to prevent his setting out on a final sea voyage. Despite the film's attractions, the book is far more compelling and manages to maintain strong human interest without resorting to sensationalism.

Anne of Ingleside

Having accomplished in *Windy Poplars* a return to the world of Anne, the author consented to still another venture into Anne's "golden years." In September 1938, she began work on her last Anne book, and, by devoting her time almost exclusively to writing, was able to complete the novel in four months. She thought of it as a potboiler written hastily for the profit assured by the popularity of Anne and her family (Gillen, 1975, 184) and did not consider it "up to" previous novels in the series (*MacMillan*, 195). The book was published in 1939 as *Anne of Ingleside*.

When Montgomery wrote this last Anne book, she had just recovered from a nervous breakdown brought on largely, she believed, by the ceaseless strain of caring for Ewan and of hiding from the world the nature of his illness (*MacMillan*, 192). The Toronto years were not happy ones, and she often remembered the peaceful days of her youth spent on her beloved island. In 1938, the year she composed *Ingleside*, she wrote to MacMillan, "Somehow this past year I have often felt very homesick for my own 'Island'" (*MacMillan*, 186). Because of this nostalgic mood and because this is not only her final Anne book but her final novel, the opening is particularly moving. Anne is paying a brief visit to Green Gables before she returns to her duties as wife and mother in Glen St. Mary: "She paused for a moment to look about her on hills and woods she had loved in olden days and still loved. Dear Avonlea! . . . Ghosts of herself met her at every turn . . . the fields she had roamed in welcomed her . . . unfading echoes of the old sweet life were all about her . . . every spot she looked upon had some lovely memory."[8]

Anne returns from Avonlea to a household of five young children, the oldest seven years of age and the youngest two.

During the course of the novel another child, Rilla, is born. More about the children than about their mother, the novel covers five years of their adventures and concentrates mainly on the unhappiness that comes even to normally happy children in the course of their development. The author's vivid memories of her own youth and that of her two sons provide convincing accounts of the fears and disappointments of childhood.

The angry resentment felt at not being permitted to do what one's peers are doing is familiar to the reader, either to the child or to the remembering adult. Jem's feeling of being unloved and mistreated and his verbal defiance of his parents when they refuse him permission to accompany other boys to the harbor to witness a tattooing ring true. The fear that one may not really be the child of one's parents comes to many young children and makes believable the plight of Nan when a chum tells her a story of exchanged babies. Anyone remembering the death of a beloved pet can sympathize with Jem's grief at the loss of Gyp. Children and adults must deal with keen disappointment when trusted friends prove untrue and can relate to Di's disillusionment with Jenny Penny and Delilah Green. Children often suffer embarrassment from situations undaunting to adults, as Rilla becomes convinced that it is shameful to be seen in public carrying a cake. The child who does not understand the actions of adults feels insecure and afraid, as does Walter when he is sent for a visit to an unfamiliar environment as the time of Rilla's birth approaches. One of Montgomery's greatest strengths, exhibited here and elsewhere, is that she remembered how it feels to be a child.

Walter's visit to the Parkers is a serious failure in parenting on the part of those model parents Anne and Gilbert, who give no reason for his being sent away. Although Anne asks Aunt Mary Maria not to frighten Walter with threats of the formidable Mrs. Parker, Anne herself does the principal frightening by not providing the child with the understanding that would have allayed his fears. Montgomery apparently held to the Victorian notion that the reproductive process was not to be discussed, at least not in books for the young. At the beginning of the novel, Susan is said to be "knitting mysterious bootees" (*AI*, 2). Anne invites Diana to visit Ingleside soon because she will "not be wanting visitors for a while" (*AI*, 8), not daring to be specific about her pregnancy even to her dearest friend. In fact, although Anne gives birth to seven children, the word *pregnant* is never used in the Anne series.

The episodic plot focuses first on one child and then another as the protagonist. Most episodes are carried over into a second, and sometimes a third or fourth, chapter, promoting suspense. At least one reader has endorsed the success of this method. Jean Little recalls the unbearable suspense she felt, at age 10, when her grandmother insisted on closing a bedtime reading session with the end of chapter 9, leaving Walter, after a six-mile walk from Lowbridge, still ignorant of whether his mother is dead or alive. Not being able to endure such suspense, Little committed the "heinous crime" of taking the book to the moonlit window and reading ahead![9]

In four episodes Anne is allowed to take center stage. She chafes under the constant complaints of an unwelcome visitor, Aunt Mary Maria; plays matchmaker to a couple already secretly engaged; writes an "obitchery" at the request of a widowed neighbor; and experiences an attack of jealousy when Gilbert is attentive to a former schoolmate. Only the last episode ends satisfactorily for Anne. Aunt Mary Maria makes the departure desired by the Ingleside family but with her feelings hurt by Anne's calling attention to her age by a birthday party. Anne's carefully planned matchmaking efforts prove redundant. The requested obituary is considered insufficiently fulsome in praise, and a doggerel verse is tacked on by the widow before its publication. In these first three episodes Anne's good intentions have ironic results. The fourth episode concludes with Anne's being assured of Gilbert's devotion, but it is filled with the irony of her misinterpretation of his words and actions. In general, the events of this last novel present a more cynical view of Anne's life than earlier novels. Ann Cowan suggests that in bringing Anne near death from pneumonia, and in picturing the depression and jealousy of her midlife crisis, Montgomery may be suspected of "murderous intentions" as she makes Anne "too feeble for any more books"![10]

Gillian Thomas uses Anne's snobbish attitude toward Di's friend Jenny Penny to illustrate the "decline" of Anne after the child has become the matron (Thomas, 1975, 38). Jenny resembles the younger Anne, being a garrulous orphan who uses her imagination as an escape from an environment of deprivation. Anne disapproves of Di's alliance with Jenny, although she gives a token objection to Susan Baker's suggestion that Di should consider Jenny "beneath her" (*AIng,* 144). When Di makes an unauthorized visit to Jenny's home, she is appalled by the evidences of poverty and neglect. Eight-year-old Di is understandably disappointed when Jenny's glamorous tales turn out to be fabrications and cannot be expected to sympathize with Jenny's need to fantasize. One would expect, however, her mother to be more understanding. There is a similar tinge of snobbishness in Nan's visit to the fisherman's village where the houses are unkempt and the children dirty and unruly. The reader is invited to consider Nan a "heroine" because of her determination to restore Cassie Thomas to her rightful place, but the title of "Miss Proudy" given her by the fishermen's children is not completely inappropriate (*AIng,* 166, 167).

Although a darker book than previous novels of the series, humor is present, based largely on the reader's understanding of matters of which the children are ignorant. Susan Baker and Cornelia Bryant Elliot appear again, each attempting to outdo the other in describing the incongruous behavior of village inhabitants.

Perhaps the strongest section of the novel is chapters 32–33. In chapter 32 a village quilting party engages in the type of humorous dialogue at which Montgomery excelled. In the following chapter, Anne recalls the funeral of the brutal, tyrannical Peter Kirk. The sister of Kirk's first wife attends the funeral and delivers a bitter exposé of the man who had just been praised as "a good husband and a kind neighbor" (*AIng,* 192). She is calmly thanked by Kirk's second wife, and Anne senses that the expressed hatred of Clara Wilson is "a pale thing" (*AIng,* 193) in comparison to the unexpressed loathing of Olivia Kirk. It is a powerful and disturbing episode, bringing before us a glimpse, unusual in a Montgomery novel, of the "pit" (*AIng,* 193) of human evil and suffering. It is unfortunate, as Gillian Thomas notes, that the tirade of Clara Wilson is "undercut" by a neighbor's explanation that Clara had once been in love with Peter Kirk. Thus, her exposé becomes not merely an expression of righteous indignation at his treatment of her sister but, in part, "the trivial vindictiveness of a jilted woman" (Thomas, 1975, 40).

Despite its humor and Anne's affirmation of happiness found in home and family, *Ingleside* is pervaded by shadows of death and sorrow. It seems to be a determined effort at cheerfulness by an unhappy writer.

Filmed for Television: The Continuing Story of Anne of Green Gables

The phenomenal success of the 1985 CBC production for television of *Anne of Green Gables* prompted Kevin Sullivan to undertake, in 1987, a sequel dealing with the older Anne. *Anne of Avonlea: The Continuing Story*, a series of four hour-long episodes, is a patchwork of material from three novels, *Anne of Avonlea*, *Anne of the Island*, and *Anne of Windy Poplars*. Most of the incidents come from *Avonlea* and *Windy Poplars*, with *Island* contributing Gilbert's rejected proposal, Anne's brief involvement with a handsome rich man who bears only slight resemblance to Royal Gardner, and the concluding incident of Gilbert's illness, Anne's recognition of her love for him, and his accepted proposal.

Although several incidents are essentially faithful to the novels, others are innovations. Happily, much of the original dialogue is retained even if incorporated into different situations. To reduce roles to a manageable number, some incidents involve participants different from those in the original, and some characters are composites of those appearing in the books.

As a writer, Montgomery is sometimes viewed as a period piece, a purveyor of Victorian sentimentality. It seems worth noting that this modern film is more sentimental and less credible than the novels on which it is based. Mrs. Harris (a composite of Sarah Pringle, Mrs. Campbell, and Mrs. Gibson of *Windy Poplars*) longs sentimentally to be united with her Josiah in the afterlife. The death scene of Thomas Lynde is dramatically portrayed, and Rachel's grief for him is more voluble than it is in

Avonlea. Katherine Brooke becomes a harder, more vindictive character, making Anne's reformation of her far less believable. In *Windy Poplars,* Anne possesses knowledge about the Pringle family, found in an old diary, that brings about the end of the feud. In the film, she uses such a weapon to influence Mrs. Harris to permit her granddaughter to be tutored, but the Pringles are conquered simply by their daughters' successful performances in Anne's school play, a sudden and unlikely capitulation for that stubborn clan. In the novel, young Jen Pringle is actually a kindred spirit influenced by her family to cause minor problems in the school. The film portrays Jen as a cruel troublemaker, and her reconciliation with Anne, simply because she desires to be a part of the school dramatic society, taxes credibility.

Incidentally, the author probably would have been less than pleased with the credit lines stating that the film is based on novels written by "Lucy Maud Montgomery." She detested the combination of her Christian names, was always called simply "Maud," and, of course, signed her writings "L. M. Montgomery."

An examination of the later Anne novels reveals a growing cynicism on the part of the author and a tendency toward a less-idyllic representation of village life. The idea that close observation of one's actions by neighbors in a small community may prove more oppressive than heartwarming is presented implicitly in earlier books. In these later novels the theme becomes more explicit. It is particularly notable in the treatment of the Meredith children in *Rainbow Valley* and in the intolerance displayed by the Pringle clan in *Windy Poplars.* Optimistic patterns recur in reunions of estranged lovers and of kin with kin, in orphans finding happy homes, and in courtships culminating in happy marriages. However, the shadows of war, death, unreasonable prejudices, and frustrated expectations become increasingly prominent.

5

"Where Airy Voices Lead": The Emily Trilogy

After completing *Rilla of Ingleside*, Montgomery wrote to George MacMillan, "I have gone completely 'stale' on Anne and *must* get a new heroine" (*MacMillan*, 103). The new heroine was Emily Byrd Starr, protagonist of Montgomery's three most autobiographical novels.

Although Emily is a new heroine, she resembles her red-haired predecessor. Both Emily and Anne are orphans living with surrogate parents who attempt to rear them by a strict Calvinist code. They are alike in their rebellious spirits, their fantasy worlds, their naming of places and objects, and their devotion to a childhood companion of the same sex, Anne to Diana and Emily to Ilse. Both dislike being different in appearance from their peers; Emily longs for a bang as Anne longs for puffed sleeves. Both eventually marry a childhood sweetheart. Emily, however, is reared by members of her own family and is both strengthened and oppressed by family traditions. Most important, the literary creativity and ambitions that are a minor part of Anne's story become a major theme in the Emily trilogy.

Emily of New Moon

Emily of New Moon begins when the 10-year-old heroine is orphaned by the loss of her beloved father and is taken to live

87

with the proud Murrays of New Moon. Before his death, her father speaks to Emily of her mother's family, the Murrays, and of Emily's rare gift and the love between her father and mother. The Murrays, he explains, came from Scotland in 1790 and are noted for their family pride, which has become a "byword along the north shore" where they are known as "the chosen people."[1] Even though Juliet Murray was never forgiven by the clan for eloping with Douglas Starr, he admits that "they have some things to be proud of" (*ENM*, 14). The dying man tells his daughter that she has inherited, in greater measure, his own creative gift and assures her that she will succeed where he has failed. Although grieved by her father's death, Emily feels that she belongs to an illustrious family and has a strong sense of her own self-hood.[2] In this story, family traditions and personal expectations often conflict, but both strengthen Emily as a person and a writer.

When Emily meets the Murray clan, which has assembled to attend her father's funeral and determine her fate, she resolves not to reveal her feelings of fear and aloneness, already showing Murray-like pride. Her independent spirit resists their attempts to dominate her, and she answers their remarks on her appearance and behavior with blunt honesty. Most of the Murrays are appalled by this ill-bred "hop out of kin" (*ENM*, 19), but Aunt Laura offers her love because Emily is her sister's child, and Cousin Jimmy applauds her defiance of the clan. In this episode, Emily exhibits not only her independent spirit but the ability of the writer to detach herself from the scene and consider recreating it on paper: "She would have given anything to be out of the room. Yet in the back of her mind a design was forming of writing all about them in the old account book. It would be interesting. She could describe them all—she knew she could" (*ENM*, 29). Again and again, Emily turns to writing as therapy for the wounds she receives from an unsympathetic society and uses opposition to her individuality and to her writing as inspiration for literary expression.

Labeled "queer" (*ENM*, 22) by her more conventional neighbors, Emily faces hostility from children as well as from adults. On her first day at the Blair Water school she is humiliated by being made to wear a gingham apron, sunbonnet, and buttoned

boots and by childish teasing. She nevertheless faces her
unfriendly schoolmates with dignity and a level gaze and tells
her tormentors, "You can say what you like about me but you
are not going to insult my family." When asked what she can do,
she replies, "I can write poetry" (*ENM*, 82–83). Here Emily is
seen to be one of the "chosen people" in two senses—as part of
an old and respected family and as one set apart with a special
gift.

Although Emily's growing sense of belonging to a family is a
source of strength, the recognized head of that family, Aunt
Elizabeth, is her principal antagonist. Aunt Elizabeth considers
Emily unacceptably odd and is determined to tyrannize her into
conformity. She is another of the domineering adults that frequent Montgomery novels and make rough the path of childhood. Emily cannot understand why children do not deserve the
same respect as adults and rebels against her aunt's unfairness.
Aunt Elizabeth insists that the child's hair must be cut, obliv-
ious to Emily's pride in her "one beauty"; Emily defies her aunt
and gives her the "Murray look," an inheritance from her grandfather (*ENM*, 110–11). Aunt Elizabeth demands that Emily
wear buttoned boots and stockings on a hot day when all her
peers are barefoot; Emily removes these encumbrances when
outside the New Moon gate. For this rebellion, Emily is locked in
the semidarkness of the ancestor-haunted spare room but
escapes through a window. When Aunt Elizabeth arranges for
her niece's kitten to be drowned, Emily rescues her pet and
again defies Aunt Elizabeth with the "Murray look." When
Emily comes into conflict with her teacher, the sharp-tongued
and hard-hearted Miss Brownell, Aunt Elizabeth refuses to hear
Emily's side of the controversy; Emily escapes the humiliation of
kneeling in penitence before her teacher only through Cousin
Jimmy's appeal to Aunt Elizabeth's strict Presbyterianism with
his cogent comment that one should kneel only before one's
Maker. Emily's defiance of adults is especially delightful to
young readers because she is often the victor in the conflict.

The most significant battles between the strong-willed
Emily and Aunt Elizabeth concern Emily's writing. To Aunt
Elizabeth, writing poetry is a foolish waste of time and unwor-
thy of a Murray of New Moon. When Elizabeth discovers that

Emily is also writing fiction, the conflict intensifies, for fiction is considered an abomination. Emily believes in herself and in her vocation and refuses to comply with her aunt's command that she write no more stories. The climax of the struggle comes when Aunt Elizabeth discovers and reads Emily's concealed letters to her dead father. When Emily ferociously maintains her right to privacy, Aunt Elizabeth realizes that children and adults should be accorded the same consideration. In the latter part of the book Emily's writing is still not approved, but Elizabeth treats her young niece with greater respect.

The reader becomes aware of Emily's growing resemblance to her major antagonist. This resemblance is not pointed out directly but unfolds gradually (Miller, 1987, 309). Emily shares with Elizabeth Murray a love of place, firmness of conviction, and truthfulness, qualities partially innate but strengthened in Emily by her aunt's example. Emily immediately responds to the beauty, dignity, and sense of the past that endear the New Moon homestead to her guardian. Aunt Elizabeth values industry, thrift, and tradition and abhors the wickedness of card playing, dancing, the theater, and novels, beliefs from which she does not waver. While not always agreeing with her aunt's opinions, Emily respects and imitates her tenacity. Aunt Elizabeth is forthright and truthful, always speaking the truth as she sees it. When Emily, ill and delirious, insists that an old well be searched for the body of Ilse's mother, she turns to Aunt Elizabeth: "'I know *you'll* keep your word,' she said. 'You are very hard—but *you* never lie, Aunt Elizabeth'" (*ENM*, 334). The example of her aunt's uncompromising truthfulness increases Emily's dislike of deception, and she rejects Aunt Laura's suggestions that she read novels "on the sly" (*ENM*, 103), that she continue to hide her boots and go barefoot, and that she conceal her story writing from Aunt Elizabeth. Although Emily responds to Laura's tenderness and affection, she is more truly the descendant of Elizabeth. Ironically, the influence of Aunt Elizabeth and the Murray traditions strengthens qualities in Emily that cause her to continue her writing, the very pursuit that the Murray clan condemns.

A part of Emily's development of sense of family and self comes from the stories of her ancestors told her by Cousin

Jimmy. The family legends of Emily's two great-great-grand-mothers come directly from tales of Montgomery's own ancestors. One story is of the settling of the Murrays on Prince Edward Island because Mary Murray refused to leave the island where the ship, from Scotland bound for Quebec, anchored for water, a refusal expressed firmly in the words "Here I stay" (*ENM*, 74). The second tale is of the woman so homesick for Scotland that for weeks she paced the floor wearing her bonnet and demanding to be taken home. The "Here I stay" woman was modeled on the author's great-great-grandmother on the Montgomery side and she of bonnet fame on a Macneill ancestor. These stories are transplanted to Emily's background and Cousin Jimmy's recounting of family legends. From such stories, as well as from the example of Aunt Elizabeth, Emily learns of the strength and independence of women and pursues her own course with an indomitable spirit worthy of her forbears.

As Emily responds appreciatively to the beauty of the ancestral homestead, revels in clan legends, and defends the family to outsiders, she steadily develops a sense of belonging to a family. She even beards a Catholic priest in his rectory to plead his appeal to a parishioner to spare the grove that protects New Moon from northern winds. When she is at last allowed "a room of her own" (*ENM*, 293), the room once occupied by her mother, she senses both a stronger bond with her mother's family and a keener awareness of her own individuality. Emily, however, does not truly belong to New Moon until the climax of the major conflict with Aunt Elizabeth. In this dramatic episode, not only the adult but the child experiences an anagnorisis. Although outraged by her aunt's invasion of her privacy, Emily grieves because she has hurt Aunt Elizabeth through the pointed description contained in the letters to her father. When Elizabeth apologizes to her niece, Emily realizes for the first time that she is loved by her aunt, that she has ceased to be merely a "duty" (*ENM*, 326). After this episode, Emily writes no more letters to her father although she now has no fear of Aunt Elizabeth's reading her "private papers" (*ENM*, 321). The narrator suggests that she has gradually outgrown the need to communicate with her father "as childhood began to emerge into girlhood" (*ENM*, 325), and this is, in part, true. The more important reason for her abandonment of the practice is left for the reader to discover between the lines. Recognizing her aunt's affection is the final step toward feeling that she belongs. She is now truly Emily of New Moon and need not reach out to the dead for the security of being loved (MacLulich, 1985, "Heroine," 16). In the meanwhile, the letters to "Mr. Douglas Starr, On the Road to Heaven" (*ENM*, 97) have served an important purpose for the reader and for Emily as a developing writer.

The story is told from the omniscient point of view, with Emily as chief viewpoint character, until chapter 9. At this point, Emily, chafing under her unjust treatment by her teacher and happily supplied by Aunt Laura with old "letter-bills" to serve as writing paper, begins her periodic epistles to her father. Approximately one-fifth of the novel is made up of these letters, and the first-person point of view allows readers to share in Emily's efforts at self-expression.

Emily's love for bookish phraseology is akin to that of Anne, and she humorously uses expressions from her reading, although her spelling is unequal to her vocabulary. Of her teacher she writes that she does not like the "cut of her jib," adding that she has learned this "naughtical frays" from Cousin Jimmy (*ENM*, 100). When she loses Aunt Laura's ring, she writes, "I wepped in my despare" (*ENM*, 160). She describes the arrival of "unexpekted company" with no cake in the house for tea as something that "never happened before in the annels of New Moon" (*ENM*, 183). Another source of humor in the letters is the unexpected aptness of some of Emily's conclusions. For example, after describing an argument with Ilse about whether one should wish to be Joan of Arc or Frances Willard, she concludes, "I would rather be Frances Willard because she is alive" (*ENM*, 161).

In addition to providing humor, the letters bring readers closer to Emily's joys and despairs and carry forward the narrative. They are also important to Emily's development as a writer, for in them she describes the world about her and its inhabitants. Emily's early literary efforts tend toward carefully rhymed and artificially expressed tributes to the beauties of nature and romantic tales of maidens immured in convents. Her letters, however, deal honestly and humorously with life in the village of Blair Water. They help her to discover and to practice her greatest skill.

The letters, as well as episodes narrated in the third person, display Emily's love of words and sensitivity to their sounds. She lists some of her favorite "lovely" words as "dingled, pearled, musk, dappled, intervales, glen, bosky, piping, shimmer, crisp, beechen, ivory" (*ENM*, 190). A line from Tennyson's "Bugle Song" so enraptures her that she forgets proper schoolroom deportment, begs her teacher to read it again, and is slapped for disrupting the classroom. Although she resents Ilse's venting of anger against her, Emily cannot help being intrigued by Ilse's creative epithets, such as "doddering hyena" and "blithering centipede" (*ENM*, 289, 242).

Emily feels that nature is alive and filled with beauty. The tall, grey-clad "Wind Woman" is her frequent companion (*ENM*, 5). Two spruces separated by a small apple tree are "Adam and Eve," and a big birch becomes "the Monarch of the Forest" (*ENM*, 1, 134).

Emily has moments of insight that she calls "the flash." L. M. Montgomery wrote of her own feeling that she was "very near a kingdom of ideal beauty" of which she sometimes seemed "to catch a glimpse" (*Journals* I, 301), a Platonic concept notably expressed in Shelley's "Hymn to Intellectual Beauty." This glimpse of ideal beauty is Emily's "flash"; it separates her from others in her society and inspires her writing. Like Anne, Emily sometimes uses writing as an escape from a drab or hostile world, but her commitment to literary expression is much stronger than Anne's. She writes because she must write; she cannot conceive of life as being endurable without her writing.

Since, as Cousin Jimmy explains, "poets are so scarce in Blair Water folks don't understand them" (*ENM*, 69), Emily encounters opposition as she pursues her vocation. Aunt Elizabeth's disapproval has already been noted. Aunt Laura is more sympathetic but incapable of understanding this strange quirk. To Laura, Emily's scribbling is a "harmless enough amusement" but "really a waste of time" that Emily might easily give up to please Aunt Elizabeth (*ENM*, 318). Emily's teacher, Miss Brownell, discovers some of her pupil's poems and reads them aloud with sarcastic asides, a performance enjoyed by most of

Emily's schoolmates since a proud Murray is made the object of ridicule.

Fortunately, however, Emily is not totally without encouragement. Among her peers she is supported by the tempestuous Ilse, by the boy artist, Teddy Kent, and by the brash hired boy, Perry Miller of Stovepipe Town. When Emily first recites one of her poems to Ilse, Ilse comments, "I guess you *are* a poetess all right," and Emily is thrilled that her "world had conceded her standing" (*ENM*, 120). Teddy must draw and can understand why Emily must write. Perry recognizes her ability without conceding that he could not do as well himself if he really tried.

Emily also finds a few supporters in adult society. Cousin Jimmy, who composes verses that he recites while boiling the pigs' potatoes, is there to sympathize and to supply blank "Jimmy-books." Father Cassidy, while knowing her youthful verses to be "trash," for the sake of the rhyme, rhythm, and one image, tells her to "keep on" (*ENM*, 210). Although Miss Brownell attempts to blast and wither Emily's talent, another teacher, Mr. Carpenter, builds it up through blunt but constructive criticism. The two teachers' names, as Elizabeth Waterston suggests, seem significant (Waterston, 1975, 19).

Montgomery is aware of her own literary strengths and weaknesses and has Mr. Carpenter condemn the purple passages, the eighteenth-century diction, and the didacticism of Emily's poetry, yet he finds 10 good lines, enough for him to encourage her to continue. When Emily, by mistake, gives Mr. Carpenter a notebook containing sketches of the inhabitants of Blair Water, her teacher, chuckling appreciatively, declares, "Why, I wouldn't have missed this for all the poetry you've written or ever will write! By gad, it's literature . . . !" (*ENM*, 349) Like Emily, Montgomery aspired to be a romantic poet but found her true vocation in comic realism.

A mystery runs through the story and provides suspense—the puzzle of Ilse's mother. Emily knows that Ilse's father neglects his daughter, does not believe in God, and dislikes women. She has heard a cryptic comment about the "trick" played on him by his wife (*ENM*, 90) and overhears a conversation in which her aunts speak of Ilse's not being forgiven "for being her mother's daughter," to Emily a completely incomprehensible statement (*ENM*, 228). When Aunt Nancy Priest tells the story of Beatrice Burnley's supposed desertion of husband and child, Emily is appalled by her first real contact with "the world's sin and sorrow" (*ENM*, 270). With this mystery solved, another mystery replaces it. Emily is convinced that a mistake has been made—that "she couldn't have done it" (*ENM*, 331)—and wants to know the real reason behind the disappearance of Ilse's mother. Near the end of the book, this mystery is solved by Emily in a version of the "flash," and the truth not only restores to Dr. Burnley his faith in his wife but binds him in affection to his daughter. Ironically, Emily's special insight both sets her apart from and links her to the community, for she occasionally, as in this incident, uses it to influence the lives of others. It is also a family link since she presumably has inherited her "second sight" from a Highland ancestor. The "flash" represents Emily's special gift and individuality along with her need to be a part of family and community.

At the end of the book, Emily, heartened by Mr. Carpenter's encouragement and warmed by the friendship of Ilse, Teddy, and Perry, who await her in Lofty John's bush, takes a new Jimmy-book and writes, "I am going to write a diary that it may be published when I die" (*ENM*, 351). This diary becomes an important narrative device in the second book of the trilogy, *Emily Climbs*.

Emily Climbs

In *Emily of New Moon*, the author left certain intriguing matters unresolved, such as the heroine's incipient romance with Teddy and her relationship with Dean Priest, who saves her life in an episode that is literally a "cliffhanger." Clearly, Montgomery planned to continue Emily's adventures but, as usual, found the writing of a sequel something of a chore. To MacMillan she wrote that the second Emily book was not "half as good as *Emily of New Moon*" and commented on her preference for using children rather than older girls as protagonists: "The second volume of a series, especially if it deals with a very young girl, is the hardest for me to write—because the public and publisher won't allow me to write of a young girl as she really is" (*MacMillan*, 118).

At the time of the letter to MacMillan, Montgomery was calling her sequel "Emily II." The eventual title, *Emily Climbs*, suggests climbing toward fame and fulfillment and alludes to a poem, "The Fringed Gentian," which impressed the young Emily. The last verse reads:

Then whisper, blossom, in thy sleep
How I may upward climb
The Alpine Path, so hard, so steep,
That leads to heights sublime.
How I may reach that far-off goal
Of true and honored fame
And write upon its shining scroll
A woman's humble name. (*ENM*, 300–301

After reading this verse, Emily had vowed to "climb the Alpine Path" (*ENM*, 301).

In her brief autobiography, Montgomery explains that she clipped "To a Fringed Gentian" from a "current magazine" and pasted it in the corner of her portfolio, viewing it as "the keynote" of her ambition (*Alpine Path*, 10). She gives no specific citation of source and author; perhaps she had forgotten. In an issue of the Montgomery newsletter, *Kindred Spirits*, Carol Gaboury reports the source of the poem to be the March 1884 issue of *Godey's Lady's Book*, where it was a part of a continued story, "Tam, the Story of a Woman," by Ella Rodman Church and Augusta De Bubna (Gaboury, 7). Maud Montgomery must have been only nine years old when she discovered the verse that served as a motto for her career. Although "The Fringed Gentian" as verse is mediocre, it indicates important features in the careers of Emily and her creator. As Thomas E. Tausky observes, the poet identifies with nature, emphasizes determination, desires recognition, and realizes the special problems of the female who strives to gain distinction.[3]

Emily is almost 14 when the second novel begins and is 17 when it ends. During these important years of adolescence, she struggles to find her way as a person and as a writer. Influences come from several directions, and she must decide which forces will shape her and which she will reject. Certainly Emily receives abundant advice; the minor character Julia Hollander with her tag expression "I would advise you"[4] is representative of all those counselors who offer direction.

Again family influence is strong. Aunt Elizabeth continues to believe that Emily's "scribbling nonsense" is a waste of time, and even gentle Aunt Laura feels that she "might be better employed" (*EC*, 2). Her aunts train Emily in the domestic arts as the proper accomplishments for a woman. Emily accepts their tutelage and even enjoys learning to sand the floor in a herringbone pattern and place pickles in a jar in the traditional New Moon arrangement. Although she complies with her aunts' direction up to a point, she continues writing in spite of their disapproval. Aunt Elizabeth even makes Emily's attendance at Shrewsbury High School contingent on a promise to give up writing, but here Emily stands firm and refuses to make such a promise. Recognizing the strength of will of both Elizabeth and Emily, Cousin Jimmy suggests a compromise. Emily should promise to write only what is literally true. This concession to Aunt Elizabeth's distrust of fiction is ultimately to Emily's advantage by teaching her restraint and focusing her attention on writing of life around her.

Emily learns more than the value of compromise from Cousin Jimmy, a man of wisdom in spite of a childhood fall down the New Moon well. When Aunt Ruth carries out her threat to lock her niece out of the house if she participates in a school play, Emily rebelliously walks the seven miles from Shrewsbury to New Moon, vowing never to return to the restrictive environment of Aunt Ruth's home. Cousin Jimmy sympathizes with her frustration but strategically reminds Emily that her grandmothers would not have relinquished so easily the chance for an education. The memory of the staunch women of Emily's ancestry gives her the strength to swallow her pride and remember priorities. "She could see them all around her—the dear, dead ladies of New Moon . . . looking down with something of contemptuous pity on their foolish, impulsive descendant" (*EC*, 140). The three years of training at Shrewsbury are important to Emily's writing, and once again the family helps her develop in the very area that is disapproved by most family members.

Cousin Jimmy also advises Emily on prudence, a quality his impulsive young cousin noticeably lacks. Going downstairs late at night to retrieve a notebook, Emily encounters Perry Miller, who carries out his threat to kiss her when the clock strikes 11. Cousin Jimmy supports Emily in the ensuing domestic court, using an incident from Aunt Ruth's past to remind that lady of the importance of family trust and support. To Emily, Cousin Jimmy privately suggests that it would have been "more prudent" not to have admitted Perry through the window. Describing prudence as a "shoddy virtue," Emily protests, "I hate to go mincing through life, afraid to take a single long step for fear of somebody watching . . . Oh, I *hate* conventions" (*EC*, 223–34). Her hatred of conventions is certainly part of Emily's charm; readers love her for hiding in the closet to eavesdrop on gossiping neighbors, for spending the night on a haystack, and for accidentally submitting to the newspaper a blistering rather than a laudatory review of a sermon. On the surface, at least, Cousin Jimmy's recommendation of prudence seems sound. A member of society cannot always walk alone and "hang consequences" (*EC*, 233). Considering, however, the unhappy effect of conventions on both the life and art of Montgomery, one wonders if Emily was well advised.

The family member who most directly and most annoyingly attempts to mold Emily to her own pattern is Aunt Ruth, who, it seems to Emily, "has all the Murray faults and none of their virtues" (*EC*, 30). It has been suggested that the choice of the name Shrewsbury for the town where Emily boards with the shrewish Aunt Ruth is particularly appropriate (Waterston, 1975, 20). But Emily learns even from Aunt Ruth. When her niece becomes the butt of unfounded gossip, Ruth Murray Dutton dons her best bonnet and goes forth to subdue the gossipers, giving Emily an unexpected object lesson in the strength of family ties and in attacking a problem head on instead of nursing one's wounds in solitude.

Emily's chief literary mentor is Mr. Carpenter. Mr. Carpenter resembles Emily's father in his abandoned literary aspirations and in his labeling himself a failure, and the fatherless girl is drawn to him and trusts his advice. She accepts as valid his criticism of her overuse of italics and her tendency to waste words but has such strong feelings and is so in love with words that she sometimes ignores these restraints, especially in her diary. When she writes a satirical obituary about a recently deceased neighbor, Mr. Carpenter agrees that the verse is clever but advises her against biting satire and takes her mockery of weakness as a personal offense. Grieved that she has hurt her teacher, Emily vows that henceforth her pen "shall heal, not hurt." She does not, however, tear up the poem; it is "too good to destroy" (*EC*, 21). Mr. Carpenter is perhaps too critical of Emily's gift for satire; she bows to his opinion but continues to recognize the worth of the condemned work. A later poem, torn to shreds by Mr. Carpenter himself, describes the fir grove in darkness when alien and unholy spirits seem to move with stealthy footfalls. Mr. Carpenter denounces the work as "sheer Paganism," with the further comment: "To be sure from the point of view of literature it's worth a thousand of your pretty songs. All the same, that way danger lies. Better stick to your own age." Emily could never have destroyed the poem. "But Mr. Carpenter was right—I feel it," she records in her diary (*EC*, 243). Was he? Judith Miller has studied the "silences" in the book, those places where the author does not speak but leaves a conclusion for careful readers. Emily feels that she should heed Mr. Carpenter's dictates but is often reluctant to do so as she struggles to find her own voice.[5] Montgomery, mindful of the conventions of her own age, especially the demands of public and publishers, may be indicating that she wishes she had gone her own way.

Emily finds another father figure in Dean Priest, who was, in fact, a schoolmate of her real father and who falls in love with her when, in *Emily of New Moon*, he saves her life. The reader is far more aware of the nature of his attachment than is Emily, a situation providing several instances of dramatic irony. Dean contributes to Emily's development as an artist by broadening the scope of her rather narrow world with stories of faraway places; by furnishing her with books; by discussing topics, such as reincarnation, that are alien to the strict Presbyterians of New Moon; and by encouraging her imagination through such

activities as finding pictures in the clouds. But Dean is possessive and is jealous of Emily's desire for education, her friendship
with Teddy Kent, and her writing ambitions. Speaking of the
possessiveness of Teddy's mother, he predicts that the young
artist may find success if his "morbid mother doesn't ruin his
life," apparently unaware that his own attitude toward Emily is
of the same nature (*EC*, 29). Delighting in Dean's conversation
and in his letters, Emily nevertheless resents his laughing
reference to her as his "property" and writes in her diary, "I am
not anybody's 'property,' not even in fun, and I *never* will be"
(*EC*, 29). Although grateful for all she has learned from Dean,
Emily is her own person.

Emily encounters another advisor in Janet Royal, a successful member of the staff of a prestigious magazine, who offers the
young writer the opportunity to go to New York as her protégé.
The initial encounter of Miss Royal and Emily is a farcical
episode in which an unruly dog is allowed to wreak havoc
because each of his two observers believes him to belong to the
other. After this unpropitious introduction, Miss Royal offers
Emily her friendship and her patronage. Emily is to live with
her mentor, who will guide her career and use her influence to
promote the young writer's success. Emily is elated by the
prospect of becoming a part of the New York literary scene but
resents the suggestion that she cannot attain success on her
own. It is significant that in the projected home of the editor and
her protégé Miss Royal's adored dog will be given an honored
place, but Emily's cats must be sacrificed, being unamenable to
discipline. Clearly, Miss Royal's relationship with Emily is to be
a possessive one, akin to the possessive friendship of Dean
Priest. Faced with a strong dilemma, Emily decides in favor of
climbing the Alpine Path in her own way and of remaining in
the environment that is so much a part of her. Following Mr.
Carpenter's advice and her own inclination, she will strive to
contribute to the literature of her own country, keeping her
"Canadian tang and flavour" (*EC*, 294). She will not leave the
dark-red roads, orchards, and fir woods of Prince Edward
Island, for, as she says, "Some fountain of living water would
dry up in my soul if I left the land I love" (*EC*, 300). Again,
Emily resists an attempt to make her other than herself. Like

her heroine, Montgomery remained in Canada, and, although she did leave the Island for Ontario, she returned periodically for times of renewal and was so welded emotionally to that environment that, essentially, she never left.

Emily's gift of second sight has two manifestations in *Emily Climbs*. In the first, she cries out to Teddy Kent to save her from the clutches of a madman during a nightmare experience in a locked church, a call heard by Teddy across the distance of a mile. The scene in the graveyard, after Teddy's response to her call, hints at the sensuality that Montgomery dared not make explicit. The letter to MacMillan in which she wrote of the difficulty of portraying young girlhood contains the comment, "Love must scarcely be hinted at—yet young girls often have some very vivid love affairs. A girl of Emily's type certainly would. But the public . . . I can't afford to damn the public. I must cater to it for awhile yet" (*MacMillan*, 118–19). Emily's sensation of "almost terrifying sweetness" is "to sense what her 'flash' was to spirit" (*EC*, 52). Her journals reveal Montgomery as a sensuous woman who knew the call of the flesh, but her description of Emily's experience in the company of Teddy remains brief and suggestive rather than explicit.

The second manifestation of Emily's psychic gift enables a family to locate a missing child, whose great-grandmother tells a story that Emily uses as the basis for her first real literary success. Thus Emily's special gift is connected both to her life in the world of human relationships and to her life as an artist. The story told by Mrs. McIntyre, "The Woman Who Spanked the King," appeals to Emily because of its humor, enhanced by Scottish dialect and its effective building to a climax. But she particularly likes the story because it is about a woman who followed her feelings without concern for public opinion, not even the opinion of the queen (Miller, 1984, 166).

Struggling to find her own way and her own voice, Emily makes some progress toward literary recognition. Rejection slips come frequently but become less devastating. Emily even learns to give such notices "the Murray look," scorning the opinion of editors and clinging to her belief in her worth and in her ultimate success (*EC*, 252). Acceptances also begin to appear, at first with meager payment or none, but by the end of the novel accompanied by checks that soften her money-conscious family's opposition to her writing. She knows that Blair Water society considers marriage the appropriate goal for a woman; Janet Royal, in spite of her successful career and large salary, is nevertheless an "old maid" and "as odd as Dick's hat-band" (*EC*, 277). Aware of the difficulty of reconciling a career with the conventional female role, Emily, in the first chapter, confides to her diary that she has made her choice: "I have made up my mind that I will never marry. I shall be *wedded to my art*" (*EC*, 5). By the end of the book, however, she dreams of silver teaspoons, hemstitched tablecloths, and marriage to Teddy Kent as well as of literary renown. When Teddy does not propose before his departure for art school, her disappointment is mingled with "a queer feeling of relief" that she still has her freedom (*EC*, 308). The book closes with Emily's looking into a pool and seeing herself as wearing a laurel crown, but her final comment is, "Perhaps Teddy was only shy!" (*EC*, 312) This conflict of allegiances finds its resolution in *Emily's Quest*.

Emily's Quest

In the third book of the trilogy, the author brings the story of Emily to a happy conclusion with the heroine successful in her chosen vocation and married to an appropriate mate. This conventional conclusion to the series was certainly a concession to public taste and expectations, but it may well reflect the author's personal conviction that the ideal life for a female artist combines a successful career with marriage to a sympathetic mate.

In *Emily's Quest*, the struggles of the young writer to achieve public acceptance continue to stimulate reader interest, but Emily's pining for Teddy, her dull succession of unacceptable suitors, and her final response to Teddy's whistle are monotonous and disappointing. To Ephraim Weber Montgomery confided that *Emily of New Moon* was written with "intense pleasure," *Emily Climbs* "not unenjoyably," but *Emily's Quest* with "reluctance and distaste." She found her effort to "marry Emily off" arduous because of her inability to write successfully "a young-girl-romantic-love story." Her problem, she believed, was her "impish sense of humour," which kept cropping up to spoil everything.[6]

Early in the book Mr. Carpenter dies, and Emily loses a supportive father for the second time. On his deathbed, Mr. Carpenter exacts from Emily the promise that she will write only to please herself with disregard for public opinion and the dictates of the critics. He then contradicts his own advice by prescribing that she avoid the ugliness of so-called realism, maintain a preference for "pine woods" over "pigsties," and practice the type of reserve that does not tell the world everything.[7]

In her own career, Montgomery shunned the naturalism of modern fiction, generally stressing the beautiful aspects of human life and insisting on happy endings. Her reserve led her to describe the sexual desires of her characters implicitly rather than explicitly. Unfortunately, she was less faithful to the first, and most important, portion of Mr. Carpenter's advice. Perhaps Emily continued to write only to please herself, but her creator too often bowed to public taste and the requests of editors. Through Emily, a self-portrait with some significant alterations, the author can express her regret that she did not always live under her "own hat" (*EQ*, 33).

Emily's "quest" is for fulfillment both as artist and woman, and a real threat to her progress in both areas is Dean Priest. Dean's green eyes indicate his jealous nature, and his slight physical deformity symbolizes the diseased possessiveness of his love for Emily. Yet to the young girl he is her "priest," her father confessor to whom she can talk freely and whose broad knowledge of the world and of books makes his opinion of her writing important. But Dean speaks of her literary efforts as "pretty cobwebs" and a "little hobby," assuring her that she can "do more with those eyes—that smile" than she can ever do with her pen (*EQ*, 41–42). The reader can see what Emily cannot, that Dean is jealous of her talent, fearing that it will interfere with her devotion to him. Her first book having been rejected by three publishers, Emily asks Dean for his judgment of the manuscript and accepts as valid his adverse criticism. She burns the manuscript but immediately regrets her sacrificial impulse. Rushing from her room in "an anguish of regret" (*EQ*, 72), she trips over a mending basket, falls down the stair, and spends weeks in bed suffering from a back injury and blood poisoning, which threatens her life. Her physical plight, as Thomas E. Tausky indicates, symbolizes danger to her soul (Tausky, 14). She has failed to believe in herself and to walk her own path, and the failure almost destroys her art. She cannot laugh or write, and the "flash" never comes. Persuading herself to be content with Dean's satisfying companionship as a substitute for true love, she becomes engaged to him, using reasoning that strongly suggests Montgomery's justification of her own marriage to Ewan Macdonald. She puts aside her writing along with her dreams of romantic love and "wild, free-flying happiness" (*EQ*, 94). Obviously Emily must free herself of Dean's stifling influence in order to be again her creative self.

A psychic experience that shows Teddy in danger is the crisis that gives Emily her freedom. Realizing that her heart belongs to another, she rejects Dean, and his confession that he has lied to her about her book frees her from remorse. The real Emily is reborn; the wind in the bush brings the "flash," and she can write again.

Emily's strong sense of family makes her seek the Murray clan's acceptance of her vocation, particularly the approval of its acknowledged leader, Aunt Elizabeth. Although the family has been mollified by the income from periodicals, Emily knows that "Aunt Elizabeth tolerated but never approved her mania for scribbling" (*EQ*, 4). In chapter 18, Emily finds a lost diamond, and Aunt Elizabeth falls down the cellar steps and breaks her leg. In *Emily of New Moon*, Cousin Jimmy recounted the Murray legend of a diamond lost over 60 years before, and one of Emily's dreams has been to find the treasure. The fulfillment of this dream coincides with Aunt Elizabeth's approval of her vocation, a romantic plot device thus becoming symbolic. While Aunt Elizabeth is confined to her bed, Emily entertains her by reading aloud stories she has written of rural characters who seem real and fascinating even to her skeptical aunt. A "witty, sparkling rill of human comedy" (*EQ*, 198) with no "silly love-making" (*EQ*, 195), the stories are expanded into a novel, and Emily counts as her greatest triumph the fact that the book causes Aunt Elizabeth to laugh. The publication and subsequent success of

The Moral of the Rose is comparable to the unexpected popularity of Montgomery's first novel, *Anne of Green Gables*. Although the book receives much critical acclaim and is praised even by Dean Priest and by Janet Royal, Emily most prizes Aunt Elizabeth's grudging comment, "Well, I never could have believed that a pack of lies could sound as much like the real truth as that book does" (*EQ*, 248).

Emily has climbed her Alpine Path, but the artist is also the woman who longs for love. Obstacles to the successful progress of romance include Emily's misunderstanding of a partially overheard conversation between Teddy and Ilse and the failure of Teddy's jealous mother to deliver to Emily an important letter. These impediments are cleared away, along with the mystery surrounding Mrs. Kent, which runs through three books. The novel closes with Emily's prospective marriage to Teddy Kent, the mate to whom her instincts bind her and an artist who understands and supports her need to write. Montgomery is kinder to Emily than she was to herself, for she allows her heroine to reject a marriage of companionship to follow her heart and, presumably, to find fulfillment as both artist and woman.

Although the book has a happy ending, the mood is often one of despair. Emily describes in her diary times of depression in which a dreadful gloom and "a great and awful weariness" settle on her soul, accompanied by "a haunting dread of the future" (*EQ*, 210), descriptions that have their counterparts in the author's journals. Dealing not only with Emily's ultimate success as writer and as woman but with her struggles toward her goals, the book does not minimize the price she pays. The entire Emily trilogy has less cheer and greater depth than the stories of Anne and demands more maturity of the reader. Emily has achieved less general popularity than has Anne but offers greater appeal to a minority, especially those who themselves have the gift and curse of the compulsion to write.

6

Other Series Heroines:
Sara Stanley and Pat Gardiner

In addition to Anne and Emily, Montgomery wrote about two other young girls as series heroines or, more exactly, sequel heroines, since each appears in two novels. *The Story Girl* (1911) and *The Golden Road* (1913) focus on Sara Stanley, a gifted young storyteller. Twenty years later Pat Gardiner appears as the protagonist of *Pat of Silver Bush* (1933) and *Mistress Pat* (1935).

The Story Girl

Set in rural Prince Edward Island before the turn of the century, *The Story Girl* tells of one happy summer in the lives of eight young denizens of the paradise of childhood. The apple orchard is a frequent setting, and in this book Montgomery explicitly states a favorite theme: that childhood is an Eden that adults—except for a favored few, the creative artists—lose.

The book begins when two boys from Toronto arrive in Carlisle, P.E.I. While their father is away on business in South America, Beverly and Felix King are to stay at the old King homestead with their relatives, including three lively cousins, Dan, Felicity, and Cecily. Another cousin, Sara Stanley, lives on the adjoining farm. She is the "Story Girl," who will regale them with enthralling tales. Their adventures also include a hired boy, Peter Craig, and a colorless but loyal young neighbor, Sara Ray. Together the eight youngsters, ranging in age from 11 to 13, roam a rural paradise of fields, woods, and orchard. The active, curious, and rather naive children await with trepidation the predicted Judgement Day, send gifts to the local witch when their cat is ill, conduct a preaching contest, and participate in other adventures and misadventures.

The plot is thin and episodic, with each adventure occupying only one or two chapters. Some suspense is generated by the mysterious contents of the blue chest of a kinswoman jilted on her wedding day, the secret room of the Awkward Man, and the question of whether Peg Bowen really is a witch. The blue chest is opened late in the book, but the other two mysteries are continued into the sequel. The story line, such as it is, is interrupted frequently by stories recounted by the Story Girl to her interested, though not uncritical, audience.

Montgomery discussed *The Story Girl* in her short autobiography, written in 1917: "It is my own favorite among my books, the one that gave me the greatest pleasure to write, the one whose characters and landscape seem most real" (*Alpine Path*, 78). This statement was made, of course, early in her career but after the publication of seven novels, including *Anne of Green Gables*. Although readers find *The Story Girl* far less compelling than the stories of Anne, Jean Little suspects that Montgomery's partiality resulted from the effortlessness with which the book must have been written (Little, 74). Plotting presented no problem, since the book is merely an anecdotal series of childhood experiences, several of which are taken from the author's memories of her own childhood. Character development did not occupy her attention for neither children nor adults change. Each child is individualized by distinguishing characteristics, and these unvarying traits are sometimes amusing and sometimes monotonous (Little, 73). Felix is fat and wants to be thin. Beverly has some skill at writing and becomes the editor of a juvenile newspaper. Dan has a practical viewpoint and a stubborn nature that resists his sister's bossiness. Felicity is pretty, a good cook, vain, unimaginative, and infuriatingly domineering. Cecily, the peacemaker and comforter, is gentle, compassionate, and delicate, "almost a carbon copy," writes Jean Little, "of Beth in *Little Women*" (Little, 73–74). Sara Ray is a youthful Niobe, constantly in tears. Peter Craig is characterized chiefly by his desire to find a secure place in society and by his unwavering admiration of the snobbish Felicity, who scorns the attentions of a hired boy.

Sara Stanley, the Story Girl, is a more complex character; she has some of the features of the typical Montgomery child-artist but ultimately is just as static as the book's other characters. Her talent is recognized from the beginning, and she experiences none of the struggles for acceptance that provide drama and intensity in the chronicles of Anne and Emily. She is like those heroines in her love of words, her personification of nature, and her flights of fancy, but she displays an unattractive smugness in her pride in her talent that makes her less appealing. Felicity, in spite of—or perhaps because of—all her faults, is a more successful character who belongs to the world of real people. When the Story Girl rhapsodizes about the moonlight, wishing for "a dress of moonshine, with stars for buttons," the reader likely sympathizes with Felicity's view that such a dress would be impractical because "you could see through it."[1]

The young Maud Montgomery loved dramatic narratives, not only those found in books but those she heard recounted by relatives and neighbors. Her great-aunt Mary Lawson was a gifted storyteller who told her about "the vivid sayings and doings" of the "Island folk" (*Alpine Path*, 16). Perhaps another reason that Montgomery wrote this book easily was that she gave the Story Girl some of her own favorite stories and a power of narration that enthralled an audience in the same manner that Montgomery hoped to captivate her readers. The Story Girl tells about 20 stories, some from books but more from local legend.

Joyce-Ione Harrington Coldwell calls attention to the value of *The Story Girl* to the student of folklore since many of Sara's stories have their origin in oral tradition.[2] Montgomery reported personal family legend to be the source of "How Betty Sherman Won a Husband," the story of the unconventional courtship of Nancy Sherman by Donald Fraser and the subsequent proposal by Betty Sherman to Donald's rival. Donald Fraser represents the author's own great-grandfather, Donald Montgomery, and the Sherman girls were Nancy and Betsy Penman, her great-grandmothers. Except for name changes, she wrote, the only alteration made to the family tale was to give Donald a horse and cutter when, in reality, his "romantic equipage" was an old wood sled drawn by a half-broken steer (*Alpine Path*, 13). It is clear that the author admired not only the audacity of Grandfather Donald but the courageous feminism of Grandmother Betsy, who spurned the conventional female role in courtship.

Another story from the author's family traditions is "The Blue Chest of Rachel Ward," based on the story of Eliza Montgomery, whose hope chest was locked when she was jilted on her wedding day. The blue chest occupied the kitchen of the Campbell home at Park Corner where young Maud often visited the family of her Uncle John and Aunt Annie and where she heard the story and speculated on the mystery of the chest's contents. Indeed, the blue chest still sits in the house at Park Corner.

A number of the short stories in the Story Girl's repertoire concern the church, the social as well as religious center of island life. Several tell of an eccentric minister, Mr. Scott, too fat to enter the pulpit door, which he declared to be made "for sperrits" while hoisting himself over the pulpit's sides. It was in Mr. Scott's church that a worshipper offered the fervent oral prayer that he might "be guided in his upsetting and downrising" (*SG*, 52). Surely such stories came from oral tradition, repeated and chuckled over by island firesides. The ghost stories, devil tales, and Indian legends with which the Story Girl thrills her audience also resemble popular island legends. If some of these are original creations, they were strongly influenced by the author's acquaintance with local folklore (Coldwell, 129).

In the narrations of the Story Girl, Montgomery uses the storyteller-audience pattern of oral tradition, which provides the impetus for the narration and records audience reactions (Coldwell, 127). Usually a story is told when the storyteller has an occasion to remember and recount a tale. For example, the devil tale of the irreverent young man marked by the hand of a black and hairy "something" is told during the twilight burning of potato stalks, a scene that reminds the children of a lurid description of hell (*SG*, 348–49). Felix interrupts the narration to ask how the mysterious "something" looked, and when the story is discussed afterwards, Dan expresses incredulity and Cecily accepts it as true because she has seen the very spruce wood where the fearful encounter supposedly occurred. The familiar locale and the Story Girl's mention of a neighbor who saw the devil's mark are, according to Coldwell, the types of detail often presented by storytellers as evidence for the truth of a folk legend (Coldwell, 130).

The Story Girl and her seven cohorts are, Montgomery insisted, "purely imaginary" characters (*Alpine Path*, 78). Artists, she believed, do not paint exactly from life but study life and use physical and personality traits of actual persons in portraits of imaginary characters (*Alpine Path*, 72). Well and Dave Nelson, Maud's orphaned cousins who spent three years at her Cavendish home, were congenial companions with whom she shared many adventures, including the incident of the "ghostly bell" recorded in *The Story Girl*. Undoubtedly the Nelsons influenced the portrayal of the boys in the book, and her lively Campbell cousins, also favorite playmates, contributed to her portrayal of the girls. Jennie (Mrs. John) Macneill of Cavendish has noted that daughters of the author's Uncle John Macneill, who lived on a neighboring farm, strongly resembled Felicity and Cecily: Lucy Macneill was known for her beauty, and Kate was a delicate girl who died in her teens.[3] To Sara Stanley, Montgomery gave her own creative gift and love of words and nature. Also, as was true of her creator, the Story Girl's mother dies when her daughter is very young, and her adored father is absent and disapproved of as a vagabond by the child's conventional guardians. Although the setting and many of the events are drawn directly from life, the characters are fictional composites, with one exception, the witch-like Peg Bowen. Peg is modeled on Mag Laird, the eccentric but harmless Cavendish character who was reputed to be a witch and was the terror of Maud's childhood. In 1917, Montgomery wrote, "With one exception I have never drawn any of my book people from life. That exception was 'Peg Bowen' in *The Story Girl*. And even then I painted the lily very freely" (*Alpine Path*, 73).

For the first time in a novel, Montgomery uses a first-person point of view. Instead of drawing readers into the children's world, however, the middle-aged man—Beverly King—who recalls the happy days of childhood speaks of "rapture swelling in our bosoms" (*SG*, 12) and of "euphonious evasions" (*SG*, 203), making readers all too conscious that the narrator is seeing children through the eyes of an adult. When Beverly tells readers that the Story Girl will attain fame as an actress, he destroys the immediacy of the childhood world. Montgomery wrote in her journal, "To childhood, as to God, *all* is present. There is neither past nor future" (*Journals* I, 362). In her treatment of point of view in this novel, she evidently forgot her own precept.

One passage in *The Story Girl* is often quoted as a statement of Montgomery's romantic, Wordsworthian view of the artist. Only children, we are told, can find the way to fairyland, and, for the majority, that route is lost with adulthood: "Only a few, who remain children at heart, can ever find that fair, lost path again. . . . The world calls them its singers and poets and artists and storytellers, but they are just people who have never forgotten the way to fairyland" (*SG*, 166).

The Story Girl closes as a cold November rain marks the end of a happy summer. With more stories to tell, with the mysteries of Peg Bowen and the secret room of the Awkward Man yet unsolved, and with four children (Sara, Peter, Felix, and Beverly) to be reunited with distant fathers, Montgomery carried the adventures of Sara Stanley and her companions into a second volume.

The Golden Road

The Golden Road takes up the account of the Story Girl and her seven cohorts at the point where the first volume closes and tells of events occurring in the following year. The dedication specifically credits Mary Lawson with being the source of "many of the tales repeated by the Story Girl." Aunt Mary had died in October 1912, at age 89, while the writing of this book was in progress.

The Golden Road was the first novel written in the Leaskdale manse and was begun in April 1912 during the author's first pregnancy, just three months before the birth of Chester. It was completed in May 1913, the intervening period having been filled not only with writing but with child rearing, cooking, housecleaning, reading papers and lecturing to the literary guild, visiting and receiving visitors, and attending innumerable missionary society meetings. It was a stressful period during which the author, in spite of her joy in motherhood, looked back with nostalgia to "the golden road of youth."[4] The book was written in "odds and ends of time" and left the author with "a disagreeable impression of 'unfinishedness'" (*MacMillan*, 67).

The closing chapters are marred by sentimentality, but the first three quarters of the book contain a more successful account of childhood and adolescence than that found in *The Story Girl*. The adult Beverly appears again as a rather pompous and didactic first-person narrator, but the Story Girl tells fewer stories, only about a dozen, which allows the principal characters to be active participants rather than passive listeners. The stories told by Sara are supplemented by those written for the children's "magazine," but these are relatively brief village anecdotes with distinctive literary styles that further characterize the youthful writers.

Jean Little has suggested that the story of the children's fear of the approaching Judgement Day is the most successful episode in *The Story Girl* because the children are active in soliciting reassurance and in pledging to reform if spared the dreaded end of the world. "Something dramatic was actually happening," writes Little, "instead of being recounted" (Little, 75). In *The Golden Road* the youngsters publish a magazine and discuss its contents. They perform in a school concert during which Sara Ray supplies the ending of a sentence in the Story Girl's recitation, mistaking a dramatic pause for a lapse of memory. In her desire for curls, Cecily uses mucilage instead of "curling-fluid" on her hair, a mistake that recalls the green hair of Anne. In an amusing episode of mistaken identity, the children mistake the governor's wife for deaf Aunt Eliza and entertain her with shouted remarks and each other with asides that are supposedly inaudible to the visitor. These and other dramatic episodes engage the reader's interest in a way that the tales of the Story Girl do not.

The young people are also involved with Peg Bowen, the reputed witch. They spend a night in Peg's hut after being lost in a snowstorm and later are embarrassed by her presence in their church pew, where she offers loud and uncomplimentary comments on members of the congregation. The mystery introduced in the earlier book, of whether Peg is truly a witch or merely an eccentric old woman, is here pursued actively by the group. They visit in her home, made cozy by an old Waterloo stove, where they are welcomed by a "witch" who brews ginger tea for the shivering Cecily and who serves them conventional if unappetizing food. But the walls of Peg's hut are virtually covered by a varied assortment of pictures and advertisements; she shares her home with six cats, a three-legged dog, a crow, and a hen; her mantel is adorned by a skull and a stuffed monkey; she smokes a pipe. According to J-I. H. Coldwell, Peg is "in the Anglo-American folk tradition of witchcraft," having gained "the reputation of witch because she is different from her neighbors" (Coldwell, 131).

The children are never sure whether Peg is truly a witch, although three actions seem to point to supernatural powers. She accurately prophesies the eminent return of Peter's father. When Cecily uses a wishbone given her by Peg and follows the prescribed ritual, her lost cat is soon recovered. Peg gives Sara Ray a cure for warts, involving a raw potato and an incantation recited under the full moon, and the warts disappear. The children are aware that coincidences do occur, but these events are difficult to explain. The question of Peg's witchcraft is left unsolved, appropriately consigned to the realm of mystery. The fascination of the unknown is understood by the Story Girl, who, in the previous book, half-regretted the opening of the mysterious blue chest, remarking, "When you know things you have to go by facts. But when you just dream about things there's nothing to hold you down" (*SG*, 363).

The second mystery carried over from the first volume—the Awkward Man and his secret room—perhaps also should have been left unsolved. Skilled in relating humorous village anecdotes but inept in recounting serious love stories, Montgomery clears up this mystery with an improbable and sentimental story of the type often used in her magazine "pot-boilers." Readers can believe in Peg Bowen's eccentric actions and the children's resulting puzzlement. They cannot believe in a man who furnishes a room for his purely imaginary dream lady, a secret that, if it had been known by his neighbors, would have been considered "mild lunacy" (*GR*, 288). Neither can readers accept the materialization of his dream in the form of a local music teacher who has the same first name as the imaginary beauty. A man who apostrophizes his sweetheart in such language as "In my dream you are standing here by me, dear. I can see you very plainly, my sweet lady, so dark and gracious, with your dark hair and your maiden eyes" (*GR*, 246–47) is not the sort of man the reader has ever known or would care to know.

Montgomery made another serious mistake in the later chapters when she brought home the Story Girl's father and presented him as an example of an artist who has remained a child at heart. Sara Stanley's strong attachment to her father, in spite of not having seen him for seven years, recalls Montgomery's love for an absent father and may appeal to the young reader who feels a strong sense of devotion to her father—a normal component of female adolescence (Waterston, 1975, 24). The fond reunion of Sara with her father may be satisfying to adolescent readers, but Blair Stanley dwells excessively on the forest's "wild heart beating against ours" and on disturbing "the rest of a white, wet naiad" who lives in a woodland spring (*GR*, 325–27). Such fanciful talk is amusing when it comes from 11-year-old Anne, but the lengthy imaginative flights of a middle-aged man are tiresome.

Montgomery wrote to George MacMillan that the last 10 chapters of *The Golden Road* were written "in a hurry and turmoil" (*MacMillan*, 67), a comment that may explain why the book breaks down near the end. To solve the mystery of the Awkward Man, the author supplies an incredible and sentimental story. To close the story with the departure of the Story Girl and the golden days of youth, she puts forth an artistic father and assigns him the purplest of passages. Montgomery wrote such effusions on natural beauty easily but, in wiser moments, with more restraint.

The days on the golden road end when Beverly and Felix prepare to return to Toronto and the Story Girl waves a last farewell as her buggy goes around a "curve in the road," a favorite Montgomery symbol. The children know that "the shadow of change" will darken their golden road and that adulthood is to remove them from the sunshine of those happy days (*GR*, 368–69).

Pat of Silver Bush

The Story Girl and *The Golden Road* were written early in Montgomery's literary career. Toward the end of that career she offered her readers another young heroine whose story continues into a second book, Pat Gardiner of Silver Bush.

Pat of Silver Bush (1933) and its sequel *Mistress Pat* (1935) were the last of the six novels written in the manse at Norval, Ontario. During the Norval years, Montgomery attempted to vary her literary output by writing two books for adults, *The Blue Castle* and *A Tangled Web*. She must have felt her attempts to break out of the "girls' book" pattern not to be completely satisfactory, for she returned to that familiar form in the stories of Pat Gardiner.

Pat differs from other Montgomery heroines: she possesses two understanding parents and four congenial siblings. Her happy family is like the one Montgomery found at the home of her Uncle John and Aunt Annie Campbell at Park Corner, and she used the name of the Campbell home, Silver Bush, for Pat's. This is the type of home that the young Montgomery longed for but found only in visits to the Campbells.

On completing *Pat of Silver Bush*, Montgomery wrote to MacMillan, "It is a story for girls of the *Anne* and *Emily* type and will probably please that public. I wrote it against time and tide and have no great expectations for it" (*MacMillan*, 162). She seems to have realized that she was repeating herself, giving one more variation on a successful formula. Pat possesses many features in common with Anne and Emily: she is considered by her associates to be a "queer" child, and she has the same passion for natural beauty, propensity for naming things, and fondness for creating a fantasy world as do Anne and Emily. In spite of these and other parallels, Pat is a less successful heroine, in part because the author is furnishing her with qualities already abundantly described; the characterization lacks the freshness found in earlier books. Also, Pat is comfortably situated with an affectionate family, and there are fewer of the child-adult conflicts that enliven earlier books. Conflicts are present as Pat resists all changes in her environment, but they lack the dramatic intensity of Anne's struggle for acceptance in Avonlea and Emily's resistance to attempts to discourage the pursuit of her vocation. Moreover, the love of nature, the personification of trees and flowers, and the dislike of change in her home environment, qualities shared by Anne and Emily, are carried to such extremes in Pat that the reader has difficulty in accepting them as sincere. A nine-year-old who fears change to the point of crying when her father cuts off his mustache and a 10-year-old who performs the evening ritual of kissing the flowers in the garden is likely to be considered "queer" by most people.

Pat is also overshadowed by the colorful Judy Plum, the Silver Bush housekeeper. Judy's humorous comments on events and her frequent narration of family and community stories form the chief attraction of the book. Her prominence certainly detracts from our interest in the character who is supposedly the protagonist and draws our attention away from the main plot. The book begins with Judy's point of view, and, as Jean Little points out, she speaks at least 50 words to Pat's one (Little, 72). Judy allows the author to indulge in the type of folksy humor that is her forte and to introduce an abundance of amusing anecdotes. Pat's thoughts and remarks are so repetitiously concerned with love of home and fear of change that Judy's humor provides the book's real momentum.

The plot is built around the idea of a child's resistance to change between ages 7 and 18. When in the first chapter Pat states that she "hates changes"[5] and when in the third chapter she prays that Silver Bush will "always be the same" (*PSB*, 24), the reader knows that such commitment to a static environment is certain to bring problems. Some of the changes Pat fears never come to pass—her sister Winnie does not go to live with Aunt Helen, for example, and her father does not move the family to the west. Other changes do occur, though, and Pat learns to accept if not to welcome them.

Acceptance of minor changes helps prepare Pat for a devastating change, the loss of her friend Bets. Bets recalls Little Eva, Beth March, and all other lovable children who die before their time, a sentimental tradition rarely employed by Montgomery. Acceptance of death is difficult, but the inalterability of natural beauty can bring comfort even in times of change.

Although Pat is not an orphan, there is one in the book: Jingle is a neglected, fatherless child abandoned by his mother. Jingle is also the gifted child of whom Montgomery was so fond of writing; his great talent is for planning houses. Of Pat it is said, "The only marked talent she had was for loving things very greatly" (*PSB*, 278).

Pleased by the favorable reception of this novel, Montgomery wrote to MacMillan, "I really put more of myself into Pat than into any other of my heroines" (*MacMillan*, 168). In view of the autobiographical nature of the Emily books, this is a surprising statement. The probable explanation is that the writer gave to Pat the domestic side of her personality, the part of herself that sincerely enjoyed needlework, cooking, housecleaning, caring for children, and gardening and had an intense interest in clothes and houses. Much of Montgomery's frustration resulted from her attempt to be equally successful as writer and homemaker. To Emily she gave her own literary ambitions; to Pat she gave the other side of her nature.

Having allowed her heroine, after her mother's serious illness, to become the mistress of Silver Bush, the author continued the activities of that domestic heroine into a second novel.

Mistress Pat

Montgomery wished to entitle her second *Pat* book *The Chatelaine of Silver Bush*, but her publishers preferred the less-pretentious title *Mistress Pat*. Divided into 11 sections, the book covers 11 years, recording the life of its heroine from age 20 to age 31, when she is rescued from spinsterhood by recognizing her love for Jingle Gordon.

Mistress Pat is carefully structured, and each of the 11 sections involves at least one alteration in life at Silver Bush. Some changes that Pat dreads either do not materialize or prove to be positive. Uncle Tom plans to marry the long-lost sweetheart of his youth and bring her to his home adjacent to Silver Bush, but both he and his Merle are disillusioned by the changes wrought by time, and Swallowfield escapes a new mistress. Montgomery's favorite reunion theme is here given a comic twist. Judy makes elaborate preparations to visit Ireland but, too greatly attached to the Silver Bush family to endure a long absence, cancels the trip. Pat fears that a new hired man will disrupt Silver Bush life, but Josiah Tillytuck fits in immediately and adds flavor to his environment. Other changes prove disruptive. The plot grows in intensity as minor changes in the earlier chapters give way to major ones such as Sid's marriage to the despicable Mae Binnie, Judy's death, and, finally, the fire that destroys Pat's beloved home.

Pat's sorrows are real but are mixed with Montgomery's characteristic humor. Judy continues to provide comic anecdotes, aphorisms, and homespun wisdom, but in this book she does not overshadow the heroine, partly because the older Pat is a more believable character and partly because Judy shares her comic role with two other characters, Josiah Tillytuck and Mrs. Binnie.

Tillytuck, the hired man who becomes a valued friend, rivals Judy in storytelling ability, and a comic conflict develops in which the two raconteurs attempt to surpass each other. Tillytuck, a master of one-upmanship, not only follows each of Judy's stories with a taller tale but claims to have witnessed almost every event Judy describes. The irrepressible Tillytuck has his repetitive phrase, "symbolically speaking," and something of the grandiloquence of Mr. Micawber in such statements as "I am not above the pleasures of the palate in moderation."[6] When Tillytuck's alienated wife appears peddling pills, liniments, and cosmetics, the reader expects another of Montgomery's reunion scenes. The couple cannot reconcile their theological differences, however, and Tillytuck flees to a fox ranch on the south shore, still stubbornly refusing to believe in predestination.

Mrs. Binnie, a frequent visitor to Silver Bush after her daughter's marriage to Sid Gardiner, is a comic fat woman and a Canadian Mrs. Malaprop. Montgomery's typical capsule characterization sums her up: "Gossip was her mother-tongue and grammar was her servant, not her master" (*MP*, 251).

In this seventeenth novel, the author's ability to invent new situations is waning, and she resurrects and adapts a number of events from earlier novels. Like Anne and Emily, Pat is long in realizing that the close friend of her childhood is her destined mate. Like Emily, she has a succession of suitors but rejects them all in spite of family pressure to marry. The preparations that are made for a renowned guest, the Countess of Melchester, who appears at an unexpected time, recall Anne's visit from Mrs. Charlotte E. Morgan. Pat's younger sister, Rae—flirtatious, fun loving, and unable to decide between two eligible suitors—is much the same character as Anne's friend Philippa Gordon and, like Philippa, falls suddenly in love with a newcomer who makes all former suitors seem insignificant. As Anne fancied herself in love with Roy Gardiner, Pat is briefly enamored of Donald Holmes but rejects his proposal in Anne's exact words to Roy: "I can't marry you. I thought I could but I can't" (*MP*, 220; *AI*, 300). Pat's engagement to David Kirk repeats Emily's betrothal to Dean Priest. David, like Dean, is an older man who offers stimulating companionship and who is physically marred; David's nerves were shattered by shell-shock during the war. Like Emily, Pat almost settles for congenial companionship as a substitute for love. Jingle, however, returns from years of study and the beginning of a successful career, and she realizes her love for him, just as his counterpart Teddy returns to bring Emily to her senses.

In spite of its repetitive nature, *Mistress Pat* is not an unsuccessful novel. Its heroine has grown into a warm adult who efficiently manages the household, shows unselfish concern for family members, and displays a sense of humor. She is still obsessed by a dislike of change, but the changes with which she bravely copes are significant ones, whereas the younger Pat sometimes annoys the reader by her concern with trivialities.

Suspense is developed as Pat repeatedly draws comfort from the inalterability of Silver Bush and its surroundings. When Silver Bush finally burns, Pat feels that she does not belong anywhere, that "her heart was like an unlighted room and nothing, she thought she knew, could ever illumine it again" (*MP*, 331). It takes the return of Jingle and his promise to build her a home by another sea to convince Pat that love makes a home of any location and that her devotion to Silver Bush has been her retreat from life rather than life itself.[7]

Mistress Pat is the rare sequel that surpasses its predecessor. Its secondary characters do not overshadow the protagonist, that protagonist is credible, and suspense builds to a satisfying conclusion.

Neither the Sara Stanley stories nor the Pat Gardiner stories are among Montgomery's strongest creations, but both contain appealing elements. They are of particular interest as examples of the early and late efforts of Montgomery as novelist.

7

Novels without Sequels

Montgomery wrote five novels that did not conform to the popular trend of serialization in books for girls: *Kilmeny of the Orchard* (1910), *The Blue Castle* (1926), *Magic for Marigold* (1929), *A Tangled Web* (1931), and *Jane of Lantern Hill* (1937). She died before writing the planned sequel to *Jane*.

Kilmeny of the Orchard

Before writing *Anne of Green Gables*, Montgomery created a romantic story of a beautiful mute girl who is wooed and won in an idyllic setting by a lover from the outside world. "Una of the Garden" was published in 1908 as a serial in an American magazine. After the author's reputation was established by the success of her first two *Anne* books, her publishers were anxious to profit from her popularity by issuing another novel in 1910 and suggested that "Una of the Garden" be expanded to book length. The task was reluctantly undertaken by the author in November 1909. Since L. C. Page wished the book completed by the end of the year, Montgomery increased the amount of time she usually spent writing, using every spare minute until she was "fairly faint from fatigue" (*Journals* I, 363). She doubted the potential for success of this third novel, noting that "it is of a very different style from the *Anne* books, and that is always a dangerous experiment with a public who have learned to expect a certain style from an author" (*MacMillan*, 49).

At the publisher's suggestion Montgomery changed the heroine's name from Una to Kilmeny, a character of Scottish folklore who is the protagonist of James Hogg's ballad "The Queen's Wake." Although not following the plot of the ballad, in which a beautiful and sinless maiden is spirited away to a land of love and light in order to preserve her purity, Montgomery retained its fairy-tale atmosphere. She also made her heroine resemble the earlier Kilmeny in her innocence, her great beauty, and her isolation from "the haunts of men." Unlike Hogg's Kilmeny, who is blessed with a beautiful voice, Montgomery's can neither speak nor sing but plays entrancing music on the violin. In a letter to MacMillan, Montgomery confessed her uncertainty as to how the unusual name should be pronounced: "Is it 'Kilmenny' or 'Kilmeeny.' Nobody on this side of the Atlantic seems to know. . . . When people ask me, 'How is the name of your heroine pronounced?' I have to admit that I don't know myself. And then they *look* at me!" (*MacMillan*, 54–55).

According to another letter to MacMillan, the idea for the plot came from an old tale the author "read somewhere" of a mute boy at the court of Alexander the Great who was shocked into speaking by seeing his father in great danger (*MacMillan*, 49). The motif was jotted down in her ever-present notebook to be developed into "Una of the Garden" and later into *Kilmeny of the Orchard*.

The story of Kilmeny is pure romance and accessible only to readers who approach it with that willing suspension of disbelief brought to fairy tales. Kilmeny, a country maiden of extraordinary beauty, innocence, and musical talent, is a P.E.I. version of the fairy princess isolated from the ordinary world and unable to speak because of a family curse. The spell can be broken only by the prince, in this case the village schoolmaster. When Kilmeny sees the schoolmaster's life threatened, she cries out to him in warning and is henceforth able to speak. The curse—the idea that "Kilmeny can't speak because her mother wouldn't"[1]—is a striking idea even if it severely taxes credibility.

The basic plot of Kilmeny is not uninteresting, but it is slight for a full-length novel. The original magazine story contained about 24,000 words; the publishers required the novel to double this number. Montgomery regretted the need for "padding," which, she felt, weakened the story (*MacMillan*, 48). She devotes approximately one tenth of the book to extolling the natural beauty of the setting, descriptions that are lavish with adjectives and betray the tendency toward ultrafine writing that Montgomery attempted to curb in later books. One section alludes to hills and woodlands "tremulous and aerial in delicate spring-time gauzes of pearl and purple" and "emerald fields basking in the sunshine"; the passage ends with a description of the tranquil ocean, which "slept bluely, and sighed in its sleep, with the murmur that rings for ever in the ear of those whose good fortune it is to have been born within the sound of it" (*KO*, 34). These authorial intrusions are images drawn from her poems and descriptive sketches and express her own reactions rather than those of her characters; they delay rather than advance the story. Although they contribute to the fairy-tale atmosphere, the descriptive passages are too frequent, too gushing, and too lengthy.

The padding deplored by the author is also evident in the abundance of physical description given to the characters, especially the heroine. When Eric first meets Kilmeny, he sees her as a Wordsworthian "phantom of delight" with jet-black hair, eyes as blue as the sea after a sunset, skin of the tint of a white rose, and "a purity that held in it no faintest stain of earthliness" (*KO*, 61–62). This initial description contains some 300 words and is supplemented by later passages totaling over a thousand words that establish Kilmeny's great beauty and innocence to the point of overkill. So lavish is the author with her descriptions, both of place and characters, that they overshadow the conversation that normally makes up the bulk of a Montgomery novel, even though well over half of the novel is made up of monologue and dialogue. The give and take of normal conversation, which enlivens typical Montgomery fiction, is infrequent. Instead, Eric soliloquizes, a convention of the Victorian popular novel; on two occasions, a character tells a story at some length with few interruptions by the listener; and Kilmeny writes on her little slate as she converses with the schoolmaster, "speeches" that sometimes run to more than a hundred words, causing the practical reader to wonder about the size of the slate and of Kilmeny's handwriting.

Stripped of its padding, the slight plot is developed well, with suspense provided by the gradual unfolding of the story of Kilmeny's past. In the first half of the book, mysteries connected with Kilmeny's background are explored. The second half introduces new elements of suspense: Neil's passionate hostility and his threat to kill the schoolmaster; Kilmeny's determination not to marry until she can speak; and Dr. Baker's diagnosis of Kilmeny's disability as psychological and his prediction that she could speak if overpowered by a sudden desire to do so. These suspenseful elements come together in the seventeenth of the 19 chapters when Neil attempts to carry out his threat and Kilmeny gains the power of speech to warn her lover.

Although carefully planning the progressive suspense of the plot, Montgomery seems to have realized that the implausible story did not belong to the real world and promoted the fairytale atmosphere by using words such as "enchanted," "bewitched," "uncanny," and "elfland." Many folk tales include magic mirrors, and Eric gives a mirror to his fairy princess that reveals her beauty to the girl who believed herself ugly, thus becoming an emblem of self-recognition. There are at least three strong resemblances between Kilmeny and the folklore heroine Snow White: the superior beauty of both is revealed by a mirror; both are injured by a female in a parental role; and both are rescued by a male admirer.

Two notable features of the book are the bitterness of Kilmeny's mother and the boy of Italian descent who is the would-be murderer. The story of Kilmeny's mother (along with the David Kirk episode in *Anne of Ingleside*, the account of the dark life of Mrs. Kent in the *Emily* books, and the plots of some of the short stories) challenges the glib assignment of Montgomery to the school of sunny idealists. Unfortunately, her portrayal of the villainous Italian youth in *Kilmeny,* her patronizing attitude toward French hired hands throughout her novels, and the fact that Anne was cheated by a German Jew suggest a certain amount of xenophobia.

Some humorous realism appears with the schoolmaster's gossipy landlord, but the book is, almost entirely, pure romance.

Montgomery was pleased that British reviewers, more "discriminating" than their American counterparts, focused on the "psychological interest and the plot development," which she saw as the novel's strongest features (*MacMillan*, 52). When Kilmeny was reprinted by Page in the 1920s, the author still found the story "interesting" but one that seemed to have been written by "somebody else" (Gillen, 1983, 80).

The Blue Castle

The Blue Castle (1926) was the first novel to be published after the author and her family relocated in Norval and her first attempt to write a book for adults. She interrupted her work on the *Emily* series to compose this story of a spinster's spirited pursuit of happiness and saw the novel as a departure from the girls' book pattern.

Although directed toward a more mature audience than earlier books, *The Blue Castle* repeats a favorite Montgomery situation; a sensitive heroine in a restrictive environment uses fantasy as a means of escape. Valancy Stirling has reached her twenty-ninth birthday when the book begins, but she is in some ways less mature than Anne or Emily, having been consistently treated by her numerous relatives as a backward, unwanted child. Her desire for beauty, excitement, and love leads her to dream of a blue castle in Spain where she receives the attentions of a succession of male admirers. Her dream world is filled with fountains, marble pillars, and gleaming staircases, elements that invite a Freudian interpretation, although it is doubtful that the author intended these features as sexual symbolism. She did, however, intend to depict her heroine's sexual frustration. Valancy longs for a home with a husband and babies. She avoids Lover's Lane, where romantic couples make her painfully aware of her loveless condition. Only after her unconventional marriage to Barney Snaith does her rosebush, which has never bloomed, burst into blossom.

Sexual frustration is a part but not the whole of Valancy's plight before her rebellion. Her relatives are domineering, insensitive, and totally lacking in humor. Her sulking mother and whining Cousin Stickles have no affection for her but strive to do their duty by dictating that she wear flannel petticoats, consume oatmeal porridge, and shun novels as reading material, and avoid the cardinal sin of idleness. Their attitude is reinforced by a host of uncles, aunts, and cousins—members of the "old-family set" of Deerwood[2]—who are anxious to remind Valancy of her insignificance, her homeliness, and her spinster-hood.

Overridden by the clan throughout her formative years, Valancy has been conditioned to believe in her own unworthi-ness, but she possesses two important qualities that her rela-tives lack—imagination and a sense of humor. The first permits her to escape from their drab world to her blue castle. The sec-ond allows her to be secretly amused by Cousin Sarah, who is "noted for the variety of her pickle recipes and for nothing else" (*BC*, 53), and by Aunt Mildred, who can "tell you the best way to do everything from cooking mushrooms to picking up a snake" (*BC*, 52).

Added to the symbolism of the unblooming rose bush is her wish for a dust pile, a symbol of Valancy's desire to achieve an independent self-hood. At the age of seven, she joins other schoolgirls in making dust piles, but hers is swept away and added to the pile of her attractive cousin, Olive. Valancy does not aspire to a larger pile than that of the other girls; she simply wants a one of her own. Recalling the childhood incident as an insecure adult, she says, "I wish that I may have one little dust-pile before I die" (*BC*, 71).

Without hope of a husband or career, Valancy seems fated to remain in her shackles without even a dust pile to call her own. After the introductory six chapters, however, Valancy finds the courage to defy her relatives, leave her prison, and begin her quest for freedom and happiness. A letter from a doctor contains the diagnosis of a heart ailment that limits her life expectancy to no more than one year. Determined to experience life before she dies, Valancy casts aside fears and inhibitions and begins to live to please herself.

In the three stages of Valancy's rebellion, her actions become increasingly shocking in the eyes of her clan. In the first stage, she hurls an ancient jar of potpourri out the window, symbolically discarding the past and freeing herself of her mother who concocted the potpourri. In further rebellion against family customs and expectations, she refuses to be rubbed with Redfern's liniment, slides down a banister, declines to play fall guy in Uncle Benjamin's unrelenting games of riddles, and disrupts a clan dinner party by expressing her opinion of their "snobocracy" (*BC*, 65). The outraged feelings of the clan at such unorthodox conduct change to horror when Valancy, in the second stage of her rebellion, leaves her home to live in a ramshackle house "in the very edge of up-back" (*BC*, 84) with Abel Gay and his dying daughter Cissy. Both Abel and Cissy are scorned by Deerwood society, Abel because of his drunken sprees and Cissy because she has borne an illegitimate child. After Cissy's death, Valancy audaciously proposes marriage to Barney Snaith, a mysterious newcomer to the area, telling him of her heart ailment and of her desire to please herself by sharing his island retreat. This third stage of her rebellion so appalls her conventional family that they determine to consider her as one dead. Valancy, who has been living on the edge of respectability, on the border of "up back," moves beyond the pale to the wilds of Muskoka and Barney's island hut.

The marriage occurs in chapter 26, approximately halfway through the novel. The remainder of the story concerns Valancy's delight in her blue castle, not the dream palace in Spain but the hut in the wilds of Ontario that she shares with a beloved husband who is also a rebel against society. She can now give up her fantasy world for a world of reality. In the second half of the book Barney's past remains mysterious, and he pursues a puzzling habit of locking himself away for hours in a shed to which Valancy is denied admittance. Suspense also comes through a melodramatic incident when Valancy catches her shoe in a railroad track as a train approaches. A series of plot contrivances brings the novel to its anticipated happy ending: the doctor's letter was intended for another patient and Valancy's heart is sound; Barney is the author of the nature books that Valancy has read with pleasure; Barney is cleared of his reputed criminal status and revealed to be the son of a millionaire; and Valancy even achieves family approval as the clan showers attention on her as a rich man's wife.

So Valancy and Barney live happily ever after, inhabitants of a castle of love and happiness. Obviously, common motifs of the fairy tale abound. Valancy is Cinderella who leaves her unpleasant family and attends a ball, in this case a country barn dance, where she is gallantly rescued from drunken revelers by her prince. She is also the ugly duckling—drab, insignificant-looking, and always dressed in brown—who blossoms into a woman asked to pose by an artist famed for painting beautiful women. Poor Barney Snaith, unshaven and overalled, is revealed to be a rich man and a famous author in a folk-tale transformation such as that found in "Beauty and the Beast" and "The Frog Prince" (Whitaker, 54). Even the device of exchanged letters by which Valancy is led to believe that she is seriously ill, one of the coincidences of *The Blue Castle* deplored by critics, is a common folk-tale motif.

Elizabeth Waterston has described *The Blue Castle* as "a fairy-tale set to a jazz tempo" (Waterston, 1975, 20–21). Written in the 1920s, the book reflects social changes occurring after World War I. Valancy and Barney roar through the village in his noisy automobile at the speed of 40 miles per hour. They go to the movies and eat hot dogs. Valancy acquires a green bathing suit that would have horrified her relatives had they seen it. Conversation includes an occasional "damn." Partly because of the spirit of the 1920s but more because this book is intended for mature readers, Montgomery looks at sexuality and vio-lence—the heroine befriends an unwed mother and is con-fronted by disorderly drunks at the country dance. The sensual nature of Valancy's attraction to Barney is strongly suggested, although the wife of the Reverend Macdonald must still preserve a proper reticence. There are no bedroom scenes, in the modern understanding of the term, but Barney and Valancy sometimes sleep outside on a bed of boughs, and she has pleasure in hear-ing his breathing as he sleeps beside her in the hut's one bed-room. After they leave the country dance together, Valancy realizes that her love for Barney is a "possession of body, soul, and mind" (*BC*, 112).

Not only do its reflection of customs of the 1920s and its sen-suality set the book to a jazz tempo, but its general lighthheart-edness makes the term appropriate. Although Cissy Gay is a pathetic figure who supplies no humor and for whom death is a welcome release, other characters are largely comic. There is Uncle Ben, with his never-ending supply of riddles and his repeated admonition "Let us be calm" (*BC*, 80–83); Cousin Georgiana, who contributes to the conversation at family gatherings the cheerful speculation as to which clan member will die next; pompous Uncle James, who is thrown into the asparagus bed by Roaring Abel; Roaring Abel Gay himself, who has five stages of drunkenness, including a theological one; and Dr. Redfern, who is bald and rheumatic in spite of having grown rich through selling remedies for these very ailments. When the repressed Valancy's tongue is loosened, her witty repartee is delightful, and the reader joins her in laughter at the absurdities she sees all about her. "The trouble with you people," she tells her clan, "is that you don't laugh enough" (*BC*, 144).

Set in the Muskoka district of Ontario, *The Blue Castle* is the only Montgomery novel without a Prince Edward Island setting. In the summer of 1922, the Macdonald family spent two weeks in Muskoka, a summer resort located 85 miles from Leaskdale. Montgomery wrote to MacMillan of Muskoka, "It is more like fairyland than any place I ever saw . . . a dream of lakes and maple woods and islands and lovely summer cottages" (*MacMillan*, 102). Characteristically, frequent descriptions of the beauty of the setting occur throughout the novel, often as quotations from the nature writings of John Foster.

In the same letter that describes her delight in Muskoka, Montgomery writes of a daydream that she experienced while alone one evening in this fairyland. In the dream, she chose a special island, built a cottage there, and assembled a house party made up entirely of "kindred spirits" who spent an "idyllic summer" swimming, fishing, and even dancing, for in her dream she was not a minister's wife. Her solitary dream was interrupted by the return of her husband and sons from a boating trip, and she left "fairyland" for "real life." (*MacMillan*, 109–10). This passage reinforces the strong wish-fulfillment element in *The Blue Castle*. As a minister's wife and role model for young readers, the author must surely have dreamed of escaping to a secluded environment where she would be joined by someone who satisfied her desire for congenial companionship and her needs as a woman. The events of *The Blue Castle* take place in "fairyland," a part of her "real life" only in her dreams.

Critical opinions of *The Blue Castle* are more varied than those of any other Montgomery novel. The author wrote to MacMillan of this division of opinion: "One says 'the best story of the year'—one says 'sentimental trash'—and there are all grades between!" (*MacMillan*, 128). Contemporary reviews praised the book for its humor and "spriteliness," but some found the story "slight and artificial" with "too many evidences of the cinema touch."[3] Modern critics, even Montgomery enthusiasts, concur. Muriel Whitaker labels the plot "pure corn" (Whitaker, 54), and Jean Little finds it "purely and simply a dream" appealing to an adolescent love of fantasy but "more literate and enchanting" than the usual popular romance (Little, 73). Helen Porter considers it the "least memorable" of the Montgomery novels with coincidences in the story line that are "hard to take," but adds that "the minor characters, like the minor characters in most of the Montgomery books, are simply terrific" (Porter, 102). On the other hand, Mollie Gillen, Montgomery's biographer, states that *The Blue Castle* remains one of her favorite books. "The plot contrivances," she writes, "are incidental to the charm of the setting and the neat and witty character portraits" (Gillen, 1983, 166).

The Blue Castle has found an overwhelmingly enthusiastic response in at least one country. The novels of Montgomery have been popular in Poland for 77 years, and a 1978 television adaptation of *The Blue Castle* was repeated by viewer demand two years later. A musical stage play based on the novel opened in 1979 with libretto by Barbara Wachowicz and Krystyna Slaska and music by Roman Czubaty. At its hundredth performance in the Musical Theatre of Wroclaw, members of the audience were so familiar with the musical that they sang the songs along with the actors, some having seen the production as many as nine times (Wachowicz, 34).

The Blue Castle recently received considerable media attention when it was found to bear strong resemblances to Colleen McCullough's best-selling novel *The Ladies of Missalonghi*, published in 1987. The suggestion of McCullough's plagiarism was first advanced by Maureen Garvie, book reviewer for the *Whig-*

Standard of Kingston, Ontario. When McCullough was contacted, she admitted to having read and loved the Montgomery books as a child but described the likenesses of her novel to *The Blue Castle* as "merely pleasant echoes."[4]

The Ladies of Missalonghi has a spinster heroine, Missy, who, like Valancy, leads a drab life, is a member of a large family of leading citizens, and always dresses in brown. Like Valancy, she finds a measure of freedom from her restricted existence in reading and in fantasizing. She consults a doctor about recurring pain in her side and chest and proposes to a rough recluse, John Smith, telling him that her death is eminent and that she wants to live before she dies. Smith, like Barney Snaith, has red hair, is rumored to be a "jailbird," has lived the life of a wanderer, and turns out to be a rich man. The setting is Australia rather than Canada, but both heroines live in resort communities. John Smith's choice of residence as "the bush" in a valley of the Blue Mountains suggests Barney Snaith's island habitat "up back," which becomes Valancy's blue castle. Individual incidents are echoed, including Valancy's studying of her appearance in the mirror, her rejection as a bridesmaid, and her subordinate relationship to a beautiful cousin of the same sex. There are even a few close parallels in wording as John Smith's joy in possessing a whole valley duplicates Barney's pride in owning a whole island. The admired cousin in each book is said to "keep all her goods in the shop window."

Although the basic plot is so similar as to make coincidence unlikely, McCullough makes important changes of her own. Missy becomes a more conniving heroine than Valancy, as she steals from the doctor's desk a letter to another patient to use as false evidence of her fatal illness. Missy's mother is strong-minded and authoritarian but loves her daughter and even encourages her growing independence. In McCullough's book, John Smith uses his wealth to free the female members of the clan from their subjection to the males, providing the book with a more obvious feminist appeal. Missy has a fairy godmother in the former wife of John Smith, who returns to life to assist the heroine. This supernatural element makes the plot of *The Ladies of Missalonghi* even more implausible than that of *The Blue Castle*.

Even though McCullough is undoubtedly indebted to Montgomery, the words of her story are, except for a few echoes, certainly her own, and only words are protected by copyright. The threat of legal action by the L. M. Montgomery estate has therefore not materialized. The gratifying element in this furor is that *The Blue Castle*, for many years out of print, has been brought into the limelight and its plot, often described as too contrived, has been shown to have lasting popular appeal.

Magic for Marigold

In the late 1920s, Montgomery published in the *Delineator* a series of short stories about a little girl named Marigold. When the periodical acquired a new editor, four Marigold stories were denied publication because of the editor's desire to print "more sophisticated" fiction (Gillen, 1983, 156). A book of Marigold's adventures was completed in 1928 and published the next year. Several of the chapters were originally designed for periodical publication, so the plot is essentially episodic, but the unifying element is a lonely child's search for companionship.

In *Magic for Marigold* the reader does not enter the point of view of the heroine until the third chapter. Earlier chapters introduce the proud Lesley clan, relate their discussion of appropriate names for the family's newest member, and describe the capitulation of Uncle Klondike to the charms of a female doctor. When Marigold does appear, at the age of six, she is immediately recognizable as a typical Montgomery creation. She is a friend of winds, trees, flowers, and, most of all, the sea. Nature is alive to her with trees "whispering in the dusk like old friends" and "the misty sea lapping gladly."[5] She loves home and family while often feeling confined by the strict Puritan code and traditions of her clan. She lives with joy and curiosity, finding the world "intr'esting," and puzzles her family by such unorthodox behavior as "staring into space with a look of rapture" (*MM*, 33), seeing sights withheld from their eyes. Most important, Marigold "makes magic" for herself by creating a fantasy world inhabited by the imaginary Sylvia, a playmate who lives in a wonderful place that other people know only as an orchard and a spruce-bush on a hill.

Marigold is the first Montgomery heroine to be supplied with a loving but ineffectual mother, a character also found in *Pat of Silver Bush* and *Jane of Lantern Hill*. Anne, Emily, Kilmeny, and the Story Girl are motherless, as was Maud Montgomery. Valancy Stirling is her only heroine saddled with a selfish, unpleasant mother. Marigold's mother is loving but weaker than her lively daughter. Jacqueline Berke has written perceptively of the "self-sufficient heroine" in popular fiction for girls. This heroine is usually motherless but may have a mother who is in some way "deactivated from normal functioning," leaving the child free to do things on her own. Such a situation has strong appeal for the adolescent reader because it enacts a Freudian fantasy "universal to adolescence": the daughter rids herself of the mother's protective and restrictive influence, is accepted on her own terms, and even reverses roles with the mother (Berke, 188–89).

Marigold's mother is "put upon," a shy, timid creature who is bossed by other members of the clan and lacks the courage to insist on naming her own child. Usually sympathetic toward Marigold's problems, she is never assertive. Although vaguely unwilling to destroy the fantasy world that gives her daughter satisfaction, she does not actively oppose Young Grandmother's attempts to do so. At age 11, not wanting to grow up to be like her mother, whom everybody bosses, Marigold chooses a foreign missionary, Dr. Violet Meriwether, as her role model. The daughter is protective of the mother, hating the portrait of the father's first wife, to whom her mother is unfavorably compared by the clan. Unlike her mother, Marigold sometimes dares to defy the dictates of Young Grandmother. She manages the household when she bakes a cake for unexpected visitors in the grandmother's and mother's absence, a situation that also occurs in *Emily of New Moon*. Marigold makes steady progress toward independence and refuses to duplicate the "put-upon" role of her mother.

Marigold's surrogate parents are Young Grandmother, who provides strict discipline, and Aunt Marigold, who furnishes sympathetic understanding. Early in the book she is also influenced by Old Grandmother, a forceful clan matriarch whom the young child fears. As the old lady approaches death, she furnishes her great-granddaughter with a view of life that affects the child even after Old Grandmother's death. The old woman, like Marigold, finds life interesting, and she gives her young descendant the dual advice to "live joyously" but to "play the game of life according to the rules." Old Grandmother becomes for Marigold the embodiment both of independent and joyous life and of the conscience that completely enjoys only those actions that abide by the basic principles of her honorable and God-fearing clan.

The chief plot thread of *Magic for Marigold* is that a child creates a fantasy world that she must abandon before achieving maturity. Marigold—loved by her family, although sometimes "squashed for her own good" (*MM*, 34)—uses her "magic" of fantasy not so much to escape unpleasant reality as to extend the boundaries of her restricted world. Her world is a land populated by adults, and she lacks the companionship of other children. She occasionally plays with May Kemp, whose mother is hired to clean out the apple barn, but May does not wash her face every day, and a bit of Montgomery snobbery surfaces once again. At school Marigold is with other children but "not of them" (*MM*, 216); no schoolmate possesses the qualities she requires for a true friend. Her imaginary playmate, Sylvia, sparked by her fancy that a windblown branch of white plum-blossom is a little girl beckoning to her, supplies Marigold with a companion.

A major conflict of the story arises from Young Grandmother's disapproval of Marigold's imaginary friend. Having no use for pretending and seeing no difference between fantasy and falsehood, the grandmother views Marigold's dream world as not only absurd but "positively wicked" (*MM*, 95). The conflict reaches its climax when Grandmother locks the orchard door, depriving Marigold of the ritual means of entering her magic world. Robbed of her fantasy, the child becomes listless, thin, and pale. A visiting professor of psychology, an old friend of the grandmother, saves the situation by explaining that Marigold's fantasies are not falsehoods but come from "a wonderful gift of creation" lost in adulthood. "It is such a pity," says Dr. Adam

Clow, "that she will lose it as she grows older—that she will forego its wonder and live, like us, in the light of common day" (*MM*, 116). This Wordsworthian view of the child as beholder of visions denied the adult is a common theme with Montgomery. For Marigold, and for most of Montgomery's fictional children, the dream must fade. Only Emily Starr and the Story Girl, the creative artists, can remain in fairyland (Fredeman, 64).

Marigold has brief and temporary contact with other children when they visit Cloud of Spruce or when she visits her numerous relatives. With these children she shares a variety of adventures, mostly comic. Although her new companions do not replace Sylvia, Marigold finds her imaginary playmate increasingly unsatisfactory. At six, Marigold regards her dream companion as the center of her world; at 10, she feels a "vague discontent with Sylvia" and almost wishes for a real playmate (*MM*, 141); at 11, she finds Sylvia "not quite as real as she had once seemed" (*MM*, 217). When Marigold is 12, with Sylvia now less vivid, she tells her secret to her new and most satisfactory friend, Budge Guest, in an effort to keep him interested in her rather than in his boy companion. Budge pronounces Sylvia "awful silly," and Marigold's dream is gone (*MM*, 322). She has "grown too old and wise for fairyland" (*MM*, 323). The loss of the "old magic" (*MM*, 327) at first brings tears, but Marigold finds another kind of magic in her renewed friendship with Budge and feels compensated for the disappearance of a comforting fantasy by a feeling of independence. In a symbolic incident, Marigold and Budge seek for the mythical Holy Grail, and Marigold is pleased to find, instead of the Grail, a long-lost teacup belonging to her grandmother. Reality has become more satisfying than fantasy. At the end of the book, Marigold stands "on her own ground" (*MM*, 328) with a hint of domestic happiness with Budge in the future.

In *Magic for Marigold*, the heroine does not, like Anne and Emily, change the adults. Although adults are very much a part of Marigold's life, the book focuses on her encounters with other children. The imaginary Sylvia has no real rival before Bernice Willis and is replaced only by Budge Guest, but Marigold's development is assisted by contacts with a succession of child companions. Gwennie and Princess Vavara bring into her life a

"wild whirl of color" (*MM*, 216) and give her the audacity occasionally to flaunt family taboos in her progress toward independence. From Mats, a practical child of the breed of Diana Barry,
she learns simple loyalty, from Bernice the importance of being
needed, and from Hip Price the value of sincerity. She is
temporarily enthralled by Paula Pengelly, who relishes her
martyr role and insists that "you have to be miserable or you
can't be good" (*MM*, 253). After seeing Paula steal a piece of
cake, Marigold realizes that a religion lacking joy is inadequate
and that people are loved not for their good deeds but for their
innate humanity. From Budge she learns, with Aunt Marigold's
guidance, to avoid possessiveness in friendship.

The colorful Princess Vavara and the mischievous Gwennie
Vincent are among what Jean Little terms Montgomery's
"exaggerated children" (Little, 76). They force their heads
between the bars of gates, drench walls with blueberry wine,
stick out their tongues at adults, and jump recklessly from apple
barn roofs. The reader does not share their thoughts or feelings,
knowing only of their outrageous actions, so there is no real
identification with these imps. For the child reader, however,
such vicarious discarding of all rules of proper conduct is enor-
mously satisfying.

In one episode, Marigold fears that her mother is planning
to remarry and experiences "bitterness of soul" (*MM*, 216). She
contemplates the unhappiness involved in leaving her family
home, the likelihood of being unwanted in a new family, and the
possibility that she may be required to change her name. Her
jealousy of the man who dares to replace her dead father is not
unlike Montgomery's resentment and dislike of the second wife
of Hugh John Montgomery. Marigold happily escapes the onus
of a stepparent, and although she eventually learns to share her
friend Budge, she never learns to share her mother's love, perhaps reflecting the author's personal bias.

A Tangled Web

Early in 1931, Montgomery completed *A Tangled Web*, her second attempt at a novel for adults and her most complex and

ambitious undertaking. As a framing device, a large family must wait a full year to learn which relative is to inherit an heirloom jug. What Elizabeth Waterston terms the "mosaic method" (1975, 21) is used in plotting, with six major stories and several minor ones being connected by the characters' desire to possess an ugly but valuable piece of crockery.

The novel appeared in the United States as *A Tangled Web* but in England as *Aunt Becky Began It* to prevent confusion with another recently published novel entitled *The Tangled Web* (Gillen, 1983, 164). Montgomery reluctantly approved the English title, although Aunt Becky dies early in the novel, for the eighty-five-year-old matriarch certainly started something when she left the inheritance of the jug uncertain for the period of a year. Aunt Becky is another of Montgomery's spirited elderly women, akin to Mrs. McIntyre of *Emily Climbs* and Old Grandmother of *Magic for Marigold*. The obituary that she writes for herself is a marvelous bit of self-portraiture that petrifies the clan with the fear that she may actually intend its publication. She introduces the folk-tale motif of the "hag guardian" of a treasure (Waterston, 1975, 21) and takes malicious pleasure in creating the complicated situation that will continue after her death.

The American title *A Tangled Web* is perhaps even more appropriate than the author intended. In the first place, it describes the humorous and ironic complications that arise in the lives of the possible heirs: those who never quarrel have heated disputes, while those who quarrel constantly make up their differences; those who use profanity purify their speech, while staid characters lapse into profanity; confirmed bachelors seek matrimony, while a spinster who has dreamed of wedded bliss rejects her suitor. In the second place, the title suggests the "genealogical tangle" of the Dark-Penhallow clan, a baffling relationship resulting from the marriage over three generations of 60 Darks to 60 Penhallows. Finally, a tangle probably not intended by the author is the shifting viewpoint that interferes with reader involvement with any one character. The reader enters the thoughts of no fewer than 65 characters and grows impatient with the problem of sorting out their positions in the clan. Even the author becomes confused, first giving the name

Crosby Penhallow to the only man really loved by Aunt Becky and later referring to him as Crosby Dark!

Not only does the shifting viewpoint produce confusion and hinder identification, but the six major plots and several sub-plots repeat familiar Montgomery themes and are by no means exceptional. As Father Cassidy once told Emily Starr, however, there are after all only seven original plots in the world (*ENM*, 206). In *A Tangled Web*, a young girl (Gay Penhallow) gives her heart to a handsome lover in spite of clan opposition, finds him fickle and unfaithful, and eventually realizes her true love for a long-time friend. A married couple (Joscelyn and Hugh Dark) are estranged for 10 years by Joscelyn's belief that she is in love with another man. They are reunited when she realizes the unworthiness of her dream man and the strength of her affection for her husband. An unloved orphan (Brian Dark) finds a happy home. A young widow (Donna Dark), who has vowed to be faithful to her dead husband, experiences a tempestuous romance. A middle-aged bachelor and spinster (Penny Dark and Margaret Penhallow) plan matrimony because it is expected of them but happily escape a condition neither really desires. Two old cronies (Big Sam and Little Sam) are separated by their disagreement over ownership of an unclothed statue, but are reconciled. All stories end happily in the typical Montgomery fashion.

Two plots, the Gay-Noel-Roger triangle and the reunion of Joscelyn and Hugh, are sometimes wearisome in their sentimentality. The 18-year-old Gay, beautiful and thoroughly romantic, rhapsodizes over her "plighted troth" to Noel[6] and, when his attentions wane, buries a rose bowl into which she has dropped petals on the evening of her engagement. Gay thoroughly exasperates not only her family but the reader in her inability to recognize her love for the worthy Roger. The melodramatic departure of Joscelyn Dark from her husband's home on the night of their wedding and her persistent love for a man seen only once create an entirely implausible situation. Joscelyn's mournful devotion to Treewolfe, the place that might have been her home, is described in at least a dozen passages and grows monotonous.

Fortunately, Montgomery injects bits of her characteristic humor into these two sentimental plots. Members of the clan

offer varying pejorative criticisms of Gay's beloved Noel, accus-
ing him of everything from inherited stubbornness to having
ears that "lie too close to his head" (*TW*, 166). The family also
offers a number of amusing theories on the reason for Joscelyn's
flight from Hugh. As in several Montgomery stories, an illness
brings a misguided individual to his or her senses, but the
automobile accident that hospitalizes Hugh has a comic twist: it
is caused when a pig escapes while its owner is quarreling with
a kinsman over the coveted jug.

Montgomery must have an orphan child even in this largely
adult world, and she pulls out all the stops for the heartbreaking
plight of little Brian Dark. We first meet Brian, not only
orphaned but illegitimate, as he is putting a bouquet of wild
flowers on his mother's grave and learn that he is lonely,
unloved, and has "never been kissed in his life" (*TW*, 122). Subsequent sections show that Brian is poorly dressed, overworked
by his unfeeling uncle, and sleeps in a cold, rat-infested loft.
Brian's plight is a sad one, but the author dwells on his
neglected condition as if readers might miss the point. When his
uncle wrings the neck of a kitten that has shown Brian affection,
the sobbing boy casts himself on his mother's grave, where he is
discovered by the spinster Margaret Penhallow. Brian is asked
to make his home with Margaret, who suffers from frustrated
motherhood, and the two live happily, one presumes, ever after.

The most satisfactory plots are the three in which humor
predominates. The basic situation of Donna Dark and Peter
Penhallow is that of Romeo and Juliet: an old feud separates
their two families. Both are reluctant lovers, Peter because his
adventurous life has no place for a woman and Donna because
she is devoted to her husband's memory. When their eyes meet,
at Aunt Becky's levee, they instantaneously fall in love and
encounter subsequent humorous complications. The match is
opposed by Donna's father, "Drowned John," so named because
he was once presumed lost at sea but who, with typical perver-
sity, returned home to admire his own tombstone, rule his
household with an iron hand, and indulge in temper tantrums
punctuated by salty language. Hoping to improve his chance to
inherit the jug, Drowned John, with great difficulty, gives up
cursing but remains just as tempestuous, his "dings" being

remarkably similar to "damns" in force and meaning. The romance is also complicated by the stubborn individualism of its two components, who plan an elopement but quarrel about the jug before their escape gets underway. Here Montgomery even allows her heroine to tell the hero to "go to hell" (*TW*, 203). The lovers' reunion and Drowned John's approval are accomplished through a parody of the rescue of the endangered maiden by her gallant knight. Peter rushes into a burning house to save the jug, rescues Donna instead, is proclaimed a hero, and has sense enough to keep the truth of his exploit to himself.

Penny Dark's reluctant courtship of Margaret Penhallow is likewise a humorous one. The 53-year-old Penny, fearing that his chance to inherit the jug will be lessened by his bachelor-hood, determines that "he would marry if it killed" him (*TW*, 211). Margaret accepts his proposal, also with the jug in mind, but both are miserable in their engagement. Penny attempts, by getting drunk, to shock Margaret into rejecting him, but ironically, he becomes sufficiently inebriated to achieve only a senti-mental haze that makes him a more soulful if less dignified suitor. Only when Margaret dares to tell him that his watch is wrong does Penny muster enough courage to break off the engagement, to the vast relief of both parties. Margaret, unlike Montgomery's usual characters and those of most popular fiction of the period, is a woman who finds happiness without marriage.

The Big Sam–Little Sam plot is the most completely humor-ous of all. The first cousins have lived together for 30 years, with occasional disagreements, but they part ways when Little Sam wins a statue of Aurora in a raffle and Big Sam demands that the "naked hussy" be removed from the house (*TW*, 160). When Little Sam insists on retaining his "genuine alabaster sta-tooette" (*TW*, 157), Big Sam leaves, and a silent war begins. Their conflict is resolved in a farcical episode in which Big Sam, caught in an opening in a sandstone headland, is rescued by Lit-tle Sam after Big Sam's promise to return home and tolerate the offending statue.

The novel is also given a comic conclusion. Dandy Dark drops Aunt Becky's letter, which names the jug's recipient, into the pig pen, where it is consumed by pigs. To prevent further squabbling, the Moon Man, a wise fool, hurls the jug toward the mantelpiece but instead strikes the head of a clan member and cures him of amnesia. The depressed Tempest Dark decides to give up longing for death and voices the novel's keynote as he says, "After all, life's worth living when a comedy like this is played out" (*TW*, 318).

Montgomery's first novel for adults, *The Blue Castle* appeals to adolescents as well as adults through its romantic Cinderella story and its account of rebellion against parental domination. *A Tangled Web*, with its complicated structure and points of view, its emphasis on older characters, and its wry humor, appeals, with reservations, only to adult readers.

Jane of Lantern Hill

Jane Stuart is the last of Montgomery's major fictional heroines. In a letter to MacMillan, the author stated, "I wrote the book because I loved it and its little heroine" (*MacMillan*, 186). Not since *Anne of Green Gables* had a book been written so completely for love rather than for money or fame.

Jane of Lantern Hill has several points of similarity to previous novels but also some significant differences. It is the only novel to use an urban setting, although less than half the book is set in Toronto. It is the only novel to deal with the effects of marital separation on a child, Jane's parents having separated early in the heroine's life. Although Jane responds to natural beauty, finds solace in a fantasy world, and excels in school compositions, she lacks the literary talent of Anne and Emily. Her interest in domestic tasks makes her more akin to Pat Gardiner, but Jane does not waste time worrying about changes in her environment; she goes her way courageously.

The fact that Jane is a less wonderful being than Anne or Emily endears her to some readers, as is pointed out by Jean Little, who cherishes Jane as one of her favorite heroines. Little notes that Jane lacks such charms as the expressive eyes of Anne or the subtle smile of Emily but is rather a gangling, clumsy fork dropper, inept at games and at schoolwork, and far too bony to be cast as an angel in the school play. "Whom do

most eleven-year-old girls see when they look in their mirrors?"
queries Little. "Anne? Emily? I saw Jane" (Little, 79).

Few authors have been as adept as Montgomery in depicting
the plight of sensitive children tyrannized over by adults, and
Jane's situation is her final and one of her strongest examples.
Grandmother Kennedy is the wicked witch who imprisons Jane
in the gloomy house within the iron fence at 60 Gay Street,
Toronto, and who poisons her granddaughter's life by constant
criticisms that undermine the child's self-confidence. Under her
grandmother's disapproving eye, Jane makes a muddle of oral
Bible reading, drops blueberry pie on the tablecloth, and cannot
remember the capital of Canada.

Names are important to Montgomery's heroines (Little, 79),
the most notable example being Anne's desire to have her name
"spelled with an e" if she cannot be called Cordelia. Jane Victoria Stuart is called "Victoria" by Grandmother Victoria Kennedy,
who wants to make her namesake comply with her own lifestyle
and expectations. Although the child prefers the name "Jane," it
is a legacy from her father's family, and the grandmother persis-
tently tries to destroy any connection between the despised
Andrew Stuart and her daughter and granddaughter. The
mother, too weak to take a stand on this or any issue, compro-
mises by calling her daughter by both names. Andrew Stuart,
early in his reunion with his daughter, says to her, "You've a
right to whatever name you like."[7] By the end of the novel, Jane
Victoria Stuart has been loved and appreciated by her father,
accepted by the Prince Edward Island villagers, and successful
in managing her father's home. She is, at last, her own valued
self, completely "Jane."

Like other lonely and repressed Montgomery children, Jane
escapes from adult injustices into a fantasy world. In her imagination she goes on voyages to the moon and dwells in a splendid,
shimmering world where she can perform useful tasks such as
polishing the silver moon, assisted by a host of "moon friends"
(*JLH*, 30). This escape route from her Toronto life is unneces-
sary in her island world where there are real companions, real
beauty in the surroundings, and real utensils to be polished.

The only flaw in Jane's idyllic island world is the presence of
Aunt Irene, and her father's uncritical trust in his sister is his

only weakness. Aunt Irene is one of Montgomery's most convincing portraits, a smooth, sweet-talking troublemaker who embodies habits resented by the young. A child does not like to be "pounced on" with embraces (*JLH*, 75) or reduced to babyhood by being called "lovey" and "childy." A child wants accomplishments to be taken seriously; Jane resents her aunt's patronizing amusement at her housekeeping and gardening. A child wants to be allowed to do things on her own; Jane is furious when Aunt Irene, laughing at her "trying to get ready for company all by herself" (*JLH*, 132), takes over as hostess at a dinner prepared by Jane for a guest. Aunt Irene and Grandmother Kennedy use two different approaches to make Jane feel that she is insignificant. Jane is inclined to prefer her grandmother's honest venom to her aunt's purring, patronizing endearments.

In spite of Aunt Irene, Jane grows in self-assurance through her successful ventures into homemaking. She copes with emergencies such as a fire on the roof and an escaped circus lion and is called "Superior Jane" by her father. Her successes are mixed with failures, however, and she learns to accept the defeats as well as the triumphs. Because of her natural talent for cookery and her observations of her grandmother's cook, Jane concocts biscuits that are never soggy and roasts that are never underdone. Her attempt at a plum pudding, however, results in a dish that even the kindly Uncle Tombstone avows "would have given the rats indigestion" (*JLH*, 116). Only the dog can eat an Irish stew into which she puts icing sugar instead of salt, and she never learns to make good doughnuts. Readers rejoice in Jane's triumphs but like her even better, and believe in her more, because she sometimes fails.

Like other young Montgomery heroines—and indeed, like a whole series of juvenile heroines for whom Spyri's *Heidi* established the pattern (Berke, 190)—Jane has a beneficial effect on adults. Not only is she instrumental in reuniting her estranged parents, but she uses her childish wisdom to persuade Aunt Elmira Bell to give up her "dying spells" (*JLH*, 243) and to encourage two spinsters to adopt her friend Jody. Mrs. Laura Lyons, who has not risen from bed for three years, is given the thrill of a lifetime and an incentive to get up when Jane leads a lion past her window. But because Jane is a real child living in a real world, she does not improve everyone she meets. Grandmother Kennedy and Aunt Irene remain just as hateful as ever, each in her own way, and Jane must learn to maintain her own self-hood in spite of them.

Robin Kennedy Stuart is Montgomery's supreme example of the ineffectual mother. A pretty social butterfly who cannot "stand up" to people (*JLH*, 26), Robin has been brainwashed by her mother and her sister-in-law into believing that her marriage is an unsalvageable failure. Her mother insists that she display no expression of love for Jane—a situation that strains the reader's credulity. Robin sends loving "signals" to Jane at the dinner table and slips into the child's room at night for conversation. Exasperating as Robin is, her weakness creates a situation with strong appeal for the young female reader. Jane achieves independence from her mother and does things on her own. She reverses roles with her mother and becomes the protector rather than the protected. After a happy summer with her father on Prince Edward Island, Jane returns to Toronto to feel "curiously protective about mother . . . as if, somehow, she must be shielded and guarded" (*JLH*, 203). Jane also becomes her father's homemaker, exchanging roles with her mother to become, in a sense, the father's wife, "the ultimate oedipal fantasy of the adolescent girl" (Berke, 195).

Montgomery's romantic preference for rural over urban life is especially notable in this book. In contrast to Toronto's iron fences and locked gates, Jane discovers on rural Prince Edward Island winding roads and open fields where she can run freely. She finds the island's night, with the soft moan of the sea, a welcome relief from the city's honking horns and glaring lights. Rural folk are friendly and neighborly, and since social strata are less rigid than in the city, Jane can enjoy the friendship of Uncle Tombstone, a local handyman, of the hired man, "Step-a-yard," and of the unkempt Snowbeam family without "being accused of low tastes" (*JLH*, 116).

Montgomery put a great deal of herself into Jane, who feels that she has found on the island her "spirit's home" (*JLH*, 231). It should be noted, however, that the urban and rural settings reflect the heroine's inner life. The island becomes Jane's special place, not just because of its rural beauty but because Jane finds there a useful role and a belief in herself.

Although Montgomery's later books tend to decline in effectiveness, *Jane of Lantern Hill* is one of her most successful. The point of view is almost exclusively Jane's, which promotes reader identification with the heroine and helps maintain suspense about the reason for the estrangement of Jane's parents, a unifying element in the novel. Jane hears varying versions of her parents' problems and wonders, as does the reader, where the truth lies. Through Jane's neighbors on the island, Montgomery adds to her gallery of comic portraits. Mrs. Meade, who speaks in malapropisms, continually supplies Jane with snacks to "stay her stomach" (*JLH*, 91, 93, 230). The placid Mrs. Jimmy John Garland is noted for "never getting upset over anything, even church suppers" (*JLH*, 140). Miss Violet and Miss Justina Titus, described by Jane as "pillows in the church," (*JLH*, 157), engage in disputes over everything from the color of sunbonnets to the proper placement of a rubber plant.

In spite of the book's strengths, however, not even the most avid Montgomery enthusiast can argue that *Jane* is without flaws. Montgomery expected readers to have difficulty in accepting the lion episode, writing to MacMillan: "I think the only chapter you won't find in keeping is the one about Jane and the lion. And yet something very like that did happen in the Maritimes years ago. Only in the real case the lion *followed* the lady who was considerably older!" (*MacMillan*, 186). Actually, the reader is ready to believe that Jane, who has admirably conquered her fear of cows, put out a roof fire, and become the able manager of her father's home, might take on the capture of an escaped circus lion. The episode that most severely weakens the story's credibility is the one in which Jane feels a "strange bond" between herself and a magazine photograph, not knowing it to be a picture of her father (*JLH*, 48). She talks to the picture, telling it her most cherished secrets, and even kisses it goodnight. Another weakness of the book is its use of the hackneyed device of reconciliation brought about by a serious illness. When Jane's life is threatened by pneumonia, her mother comes to the island and joins her father at Jane's bedside, creating the opportunity for the couple to resolve misunderstandings. "Superior

Jane," adept in solving other problems, might well have engineered this reconciliation without the author's use of such a stale contrivance.

The five novels without sequels are among the least known of the Montgomery novels, overshadowed as they have been by the stories of Anne and, to a lesser extent, of Emily. *The Blue Castle* is enjoying renewed popularity, and a 1990 Kevin Sullivan production drew public attention to *Jane of Lantern Hill*. The film, *Lantern Hill*, bears little resemblance, however, to Montgomery's story beyond the opening situation of the heroine and becomes a ghost story that is far more melodramatic and implausible than the original. Criticism of these novels has been sparse, although Jean Little has contributed a delightful article on Jane, and Jane Cowan Fredeman has written perceptively of the fantasy worlds of Marigold and Valancy. Closer attention is due this portion of the Montgomery canon.

The five novels were written between 1910 and 1937 and illustrate a movement from the romanticism of *Kilmeny* to the social realism of the later books. Motherhood is decreasingly idealized after the *Anne* series. Montgomery tended to glorify a relationship she never knew as a daughter, but her experiences as a parent seem to have taught her that mothers are not always perfect.

Adult relatives tend to be unpleasant and unredeemable in the later novels, particularly Jane's Grandmother Kennedy. Still writing for the child within her who suffered from adult misunderstanding, Montgomery shows greater bitterness toward tyrannical adults in her later works. She told her own story of the struggles of the artist in the Emily trilogy and turns in these books to the development of less career-minded heroines. As in all her books, the qualities most highly prized by Montgomery are imagination and a sense of humor.

8

Short Stories and Poems

The notebooks of Montgomery record the titles of over 500 short stories sold to magazines during her career,[1] many of which she frankly labeled "hack work" (*Weber*, 79). During her lifetime two collections were published. *Chronicles of Avonlea* appeared in 1912 with her permission, but the 1920 publication of *Further Chronicles of Avonlea* became the subject of a nine-year lawsuit against the publisher. *The Road to Yesterday* was a posthumous publication, the manuscript having been found by Dr. E. Stuart Macdonald among his mother's papers. In 1979, Catherine McLay selected and edited 14 stories from periodicals for a volume entitled *The Doctor's Sweetheart and Other Stories*. Through her extensive bibliographical research on Montgomery's stories and poems, Rea Wilmshurst has discovered almost 400 stories published in periodicals between 1885 and 1941 and not since reprinted. In her ongoing project of reissuing these stories, Wilmshurst has edited three volumes: *Akin to Anne: Tales of Other Orphans* (1988), *Along the Shore: Tales by the Sea* (1989), and *Among the Shadows: Tales from the Darker Side* (1990).

Prior to 1896, the young Montgomery concentrated mainly on writing verse. The publication of a few poems brought encouragement but no financial reward. In February 1896, *Golden Days*, a Philadelphia juvenile magazine, accepted the story "Our Charivari" and sent the author $5, her first payment for literary efforts. Realizing the larger and more profitable market for fiction, she turned her natural storytelling ability more and more to the composition of prose.

Chronicles of Avonlea

Montgomery's short fiction gained increasing acceptance, at first largely by Sunday school publications and juvenile magazines and later by more prestigious periodicals. After the success of the first two *Anne* books, her publishers suggested a short-story collection composed of pieces written for magazines but rewritten with an Avonlea setting and references to the popular Anne. The author did not "care greatly" for this task (*Journals* II, 94), but she painstakingly revised her work and was pleased that *Chronicles of Avonlea* received favorable reviews, although the stories had become "very stale" to her (*Journals* II, 98).

Four of the twelve stories in *Chronicles of Avonlea* are set in Avonlea, and the others are placed in the nearby villages of Spencervale, Carmody, Grafton, and White Sands. Anne Shirley is mentioned in four, appears briefly in two others, and is a major character only in "The Hurrying of Ludovic," where she uses her matchmaking skills to persuade a procrastinating suitor to propose marriage after a 15-year courtship.

All the stories are love stories, but only half are concerned with love between the sexes culminating in marriage. Others depict the love of an older person for a younger one. In all the stories, love is seen as a powerful force, described in "Old Lady Lloyd," as a "great miracle-worker."[2] In this story, love conquers the old lady's stubborn pride. In "The Miracle at Carmody," love causes the lame to walk; in "The Courting of Prissy Strong," love strengthens the will of the meek Prissy, whose disposition belies her name; and in "The Quarantine at Alexander Abraham's," love overcomes the bias of an inveterate man hater. In "Aunt Olivia's Beau," love enables the "painfully neat" spinster (*CA*, 177) to alter the habits of a lifetime, and in "The Hurrying of Ludovic," love conquers the lethargy of the non-speedy Ludovic Speed. Old wounds are healed by the power of love in "The End of a Quarrel" and in "The Winning of Lucinda," both of which exemplify Montgomery's favorite reconciliation theme.

The six stories that end conventionally in marriage are not concerned with the blooming of young love. All feature protagonists who are middle-aged or at least beyond their twenties. Montgomery's fondness for writing of the courtship of mature lovers is perhaps related to her own late marriage. Her fiction customarily uses marriage as the ultimate female goal, but her characters do not seek it without weighing the consequences (McLay, 14). The spinster of "Aunt Olivia's Beau" welcomes the idea of marriage "in the abstract" but has difficulty in accepting the institution "in the concrete" (*CA*, 191) when the muddy boots, cigar ashes, and general untidiness of Mr. Malcolm MacPherson are involved. Nancy Rogerson of "The End of a Quarrel" has a successful career as a nurse and does not pine for the man with whom she quarreled 20 years ago "over a question of syntax" (*CA*, 295), but she reassesses and reembraces the true affection of the still-ungrammatical Peter. The self-sufficient feminist heroine of "The Quarantine at Alexander Abraham's" must lay aside her fierce independence and contempt for men in order to relieve her lonely existence. The title character of "The Courtship of Prissy Strong" must weigh loyalty to family against loyalty to her heart and her desire for a home in which she, not her sister, is the mistress. In these stories, then, marriage comes as the result of considered choices by a mature women.[3]

The least successful stories are those dominated by sentimentality and didacticism, but even these are relieved by some of Montgomery's comic realism. The longest story, "Old Lady Lloyd," sentimentally describes the old lady's lonely condition and her sacrificial devotion to the young girl who might have been her daughter. Its explicit message is that love can conquer pride. The humorous comments of the villagers on the old lady's lifestyle are realistic, however, and their ignorance of her poverty ironically illustrates the nature of appearance versus reality. Montgomery here resembles her character Nancy in "The End of a Quarrel," of whom she writes, "Sentiment and humour had always waged an equal contest in Nancy's nature" (*CA*, 304).

The most successful stories are those in which humor wins the contest. Angelina Peter MacPherson, the first-person narrator of "The Quarantine at Alexander Abraham's," is determined, decisive, tactless, and contemptuous of men, and she proudly emphasizes these qualities by saying repeatedly, "I am noted for that." When forced by a quarantine to share the quarters of an avowed misogynist, Alexander Abraham, she wins his heart as surely as her cat, in a farcical episode, conquers Alexander's dog. In "The Courting of Prissy Strong," another middle-aged narrator engineers a wedding ceremony in which the bride, locked in the house by her domineering sister, reaches out a window to clasp hands with the groom, who stands on a ladder.

In "Aunt Olivia's Beau," the courtship includes Aunt Olivia's rejection of her boisterous, untidy lover because his ways are not her ways; her four reiterations of "I cannot marry you, Mr. MacPherson"; her frenzied realization of her mistake; and a wild buggy ride toward reunion. The reconciliation of the title character of "The Winning of Lucinda" with her estranged lover also contains a farcical episode. After being dropped into a brook by her gallant but stubborn suitor, Lucinda breaks her long-standing silence with the unromantic utterances, "You d——d idiot!" (CA, 152). Another romance is precipitated through the machination of Anne Shirley in "The Hurrying of Ludovic." The dilatory Mr. Speed uncharacteristically leaps from his pew when his Theodora enters the church with another man and retains his new momentum long enough to ask his lady, "plump and plain," to marry him (CA, 16).

Since the protagonists of all these stories are beyond the first blush of youth, Montgomery gives free rein to her talent for incongruous situations and idiomatic dialogue. Evidently she agrees with the narrator of "Aunt Olivia's Beau," who states: "Only youth can be sentimental without being mirth-provoking" (CA, 181).

Further Chronicles of Avonlea

Montgomery considered *Further Chronicles of Avonlea* to be her "illegitimate offspring" (*MacMillan*, 124). In spite of her objections, L. C. Page insisted on publishing the stories the company had been holding for eight years—those not included in *Chronicles of Avonlea*. Montgomery always spoke scornfully of these 15 stories, describing them to MacMillan as "poor stuff" (*MacMillan*, 142). They exhibit her tendency toward sentimentality, didacticism, overuse of coincidence, and grandiloquent language. Plots are built on situations so frequently employed by the author (unfortunate promises, reconciliation of the estranged, an orphan seeking a home) that they become trite and predictable.

In spite of their use of hackneyed situations, the stories are not without interest. Two Gothic tales, "The Return of Hester" and "The Dream Child," deal with psychic experience, reflecting the author's strong interest in psychic phenomena. Montgomery's ironic perspective on life is evident in several stories. Humor in "Aunt Cynthia's Persian Cat" arises largely from the purchase by two sisters of a cat that they do not want and that, although supposedly lost, has never left their house. In "The Education of Betty," dramatic irony results when the narrator is late in realizing what the reader early perceives—that his love for Betty has ceased to be merely paternal. In "The Little Brown Book of Miss Emily," Anne Shirley makes an ironic misjudgment—that an unattractive spinster could never have had a lover—only to have the deceased Miss Emily's journal reveal the reality behind the appearance. Three stories—"The Brother Who Failed," "Only a Common Fellow," and "Sara's Way"—center around the Browningesque paradox that apparent failure may be true success.

Not least among the ironies of *Further Chronicles* is that the most successful story makes the most blatant use of coincidence: Cecil Fenwick, an imaginary lover concocted by the narrator of "The Materializing of Cecil," actually turns up in Avonlea with the same name, profession, and background as his imaginary predecessor. To the narrator it is "Providence," and Cecil terms it "predestination." The reader is willing to suspend disbelief, in part because the coincidence is so admittedly absurd but, to a greater degree, because the narrator is a believable person. She has lied about having a lover because Avonlea has ridiculed her single condition, she understandably wishes just once in her life to make "a sensation,"[4] and she suffers keenly when her one moment of daring seems likely to lead to humiliation.

The final story in the volume, "Tannis of the Flats," merits attention since it represents Montgomery's only use of a western Canadian setting. As a teenager the author once visited her father's residence in Prince Albert, Saskatchewan. "Tannis of the Flats" is a melodramatic story involving a hero, Carey, who is fatally injured in a drunken brawl and an Indian girl's wild horseback ride through wind and rain to bring her rival, a white girl, to Carey's deathbed. Montgomery's distrust of those not of British descent is evident once again. Tannis, half-Indian, has acquired some white ways but is controlled by primitive passions. Yet Tannis joins the host of Montgomery women who perform acts of noble self-sacrifice. Perhaps the author saw this as possible because of the trace of Scottish blood inherited by the "breed" girl from a great-grandmother.

The Road to Yesterday

The Road to Yesterday, published posthumously, is a collection of 14 stories. The original manuscript was titled *The Blythes Are Quoted* and was divided into two parts, each opening with a description of the Blythe family gathered at their fireside to listen to stories and poems. The published volume omits the descriptive introductions, rearranges the stories, omits all but one of the poems, and borrows its title from one of the stories.[5]

Although members of the Blythe family appear in only five of the stories, and there not in major roles, the characters in all the stories frequently refer to Anne, Gilbert, and their offspring in words of high praise. Indeed, the stellar virtues of the Blythes become wearisome to the reader, as they are to Penelope Craig, of "Penelope Struts Her Theories," who "felt that she would scream if the Blythes were mentioned again."[6] Set in the area of Glen St. Mary and chronologically arranged, the stories cover a time span of more than 40 years.

Several tales exhibit Montgomery's favorite plot elements —a lonely orphan who finds a happy home, romance experienced by the middle-aged, and happy reunion after long separation. Yet the overall impression is that the author's optimistic approach to life has darkened. Five stories have the Gothic element of an old, gloomy house; in two of these houses a death occurs, and one is inhabited by a madwoman. John R. Sorfleet notes the presence of "certain realistic events not commonly considered to be a part of Montgomery's fictional world." He cites as an example "A Commonplace Woman" in which a woman gives birth to an illegitimate daughter, murders the daughter's brutal husband, and dies in contentment at the age of 85 without feeling the slightest twinge of guilt. "This is a far cry," writes Sorfleet, "from the Sunday-school fiction of Montgomery's early career" (Sorfleet, 1975, 6).

Point of view is treated differently in this collection as well, with fewer authorial intrusions than in Montgomery's earlier fiction. No story uses a first-person narrator, but the thoughts of the characters are featured, with the storyteller relegated to the background. A particularly interesting treatment of point of view is found in "Here Comes the Bride," where 14 individuals, either guests or members of the wedding party, react to a marriage and whet reader curiosity as to the truth. "Retribution," a dark story told almost entirely from the viewpoint of a disturbed and embittered woman, leaves the reader wondering about the truth behind the web of adultery and illegitimacy perceived by the jaundiced eye of the chief character.

Using the viewpoint of the characters makes possible the dramatic irony present in several of the stories. Others are built on ironic situations. Two of these, "The Pot and the Kettle" and "Brother Beware," use the idea of a trickster who is tricked. Another, "Reconciliation," involves a forgiver who is forgiven and is infuriated thereby. One of the most humorous, "A Dream Come True," introduces a Miniver Cheevy character who longs for exciting adventures. After a nocturnal excursion in a motorcar driven by a madwoman and a confrontation with bank robbers, however, he rejects thrills in favor of his ordinary, humdrum life. In this story, and in several others, incongruous situations and characters provoke smiles, but humor tends to be wrier and less exuberant than is customary in Montgomery's fiction, reflecting the growing unhappiness of the author's later years.

The Doctor's Sweetheart and Other Stories

The Doctor's Sweetheart and Other Stories is a collection com-
piled by Catherine McLay after a search through files of popular
periodicals. Most are examples of Montgomery's early magazine
fiction, five predating *Anne of Green Gables* and seven others
belonging to the decade following the author's first success.
For the most part, these stories deal with courtship and end
with marriage, the basic plot of romantic comedy (McLay, 14).
The narrator of "The Finished Story," himself a "magazine
scribbler," states the essence of this plot: "The hero loved the
heroine and she loved him. There was no reason why he should
not love her, but there was a reason why he could not marry
her."[7] In four stories the obstacle to marriage is family disapproval, and in six the qualities of the characters—pride, stubbornness, misplaced loyalty, or desire for independence—delay
the union. Two stories, "Kismet" and "Emily's Husband," culmi-
nate in the renewal of a marriage broken by separation. In
another, "Parting of the Ways," a woman is on the point of
leaving a husband described by villagers as a "grovelling cad"
(*DS*, 67), but decides to remain with the unsympathetic mate. In
the fictional world of Montgomery, as in the author's own life,
marriage, even a bad marriage, is not to be broken.

Here, as in other works, illness is frequently the catalyst
that precipitates a reunion; four of the stories make use of this
device. Fainting spells and bouts with typhoid and pneumonia
lead many Montgomery characters to the arms of their true
lovers.

Two stories are parodies of the typical romance plot. In "The
Girl and the Wild Race" two rivals undertake a quest to win a
fair lady who has promised her hand to the first who asks her.
But the rustic knights dash across rugged terrain in sleighs
pulled by farm horses rather than on gallant chargers. The race
culminates in Aunt Theodora's dropping her milking pail,
admitting that she has been "stumped," and finding comfort in
the fact that her niece "won't be an old maid" (*DS*, 57). In "By
Grace of Julius Caesar" the middle-aged narrator finds herself
in the ridiculous plight of being trapped on a farmhouse roof

with the ladder of escape removed by the homeowner, who requires marriage as a condition of rescue. Her stubborn independence, the romance obstacle, is conquered by the broiling sun, thirst, unpalatable food, the prospect of her new hat's being ruined by rain, and the realization that she "hadn't any real objection" to marrying Isaac after all (*DS*, 86).

Some of the stories furnished incidents and even passages of dialogue for later novels. "I Know a Secret," the adventure in which young Jane Lawrence is threatened by a loss of identity, reappears virtually intact as a chapter about Nan Blythe in *Anne of Ingleside*. The publication of "Abel and His Great Adventure" in the February 1917 issue of *Canadian Magazine* is something of a puzzle. Abel is strikingly similar to Captain Jim of *Anne's House of Dreams*, and they share many nearly identical speeches. The story of "Abel" appeared while the author was reading the proofs for *Anne's House of Dreams*, certainly an unusual publishing decision.

Akin to Anne: Tales of Other Orphans

For a 1988 publication, Rea Wilmshurst collected 19 tales of orphans, originally printed in 14 different periodicals. Most are early efforts: 13 predate *Anne of Green Gables*.

Orphanhood is a condition without age limits, as Montgomery well knew. Reared by repressive grandparents after being left motherless at the age of two, she had little contact with her father, who settled in the west and died when his daughter was 25. Marriage, motherhood, and literary success never erased the feeling of being an orphan. In 1920, after seven successful novels, she wrote: "At heart I am still the snubbed little girl of years ago who was constantly made to feel by all the grown-up denizens of her small world that she was of no importance whatever to any living creature" (*Journals* II, 391). Haunted by a sense of loneliness, L. M. Montgomery essentially remained an orphan all her life.

Young children are the unloved orphans in seven of the stories. They are appropriately pitiful but no more so than the older orphans who outnumber them—lonely students in high school or college, young women forced to pursue uncongenial employment, and even one elderly woman deprived of contact with her family. Some of the children and young people find homes with sympathetic adults with whom there is no blood kinship. The majority, however, discover, by amazing coincidences, relatives previously unknown to them.

Most of these characters escape from poverty in their new homes, but material prosperity is always secondary to being loved.[8] For some, physical needs are amply supplied, but love and understanding are absent. In "Charlotte's Quest," the title character lives with relatives who "dress her up like a doll," but she knows that she is considered a "queer" child and a misfit in the clan.[9] Living in an affluent household, little Joyce ("The Little Black Doll") feels loved only by a French servant girl. Talented orphans look forward to nurturing their gifts in a new environment, but love is their greatest need. In "Ted's Afternoon Off," a young violinist accepts a new home with an adoptive father and the promise of a musical education but explains, "But it isn't so much because of the music—it's because I love you" (*Akin*, 71). Orphans may be poor, and often are, but love rather than money opens the door out of orphanhood.

Most of these stories were designed for juvenile, religious publications—the Sunday-school papers that were the principal market for Montgomery's early fiction. Stories written for such a market, she explained, must contain a moral, "broad or subtle," to sell (*Alpine Path*, 61). In the stories of this volume, virtue is immediately rewarded, almost always by providing an orphan with a loving home. Unselfish kindness toward others, the stellar virtue around which 10 stories center, is emphasized. Those who sacrifice for others—whether they sacrifice a Sunday-school picnic ("Ted's Afternoon Off"), a prized doll ("The Little Black Doll"), or a trip to Vancouver ("Margaret's Patient")—receive their reward. Such self-renunciation does not come easily, so the principal conflict takes the form of an internal struggle. Sometimes the performer of the kind act wins the prize of a happy home, but sometimes, as in five stories, this reward comes to the recipient of the kindness. The unselfish agent gains the less tangible, but no less valuable, rewards of right action and joy in another's happiness. Blatant didacticism is generally avoided by having the characters, rather than the preaching author, reflect on the moral lessons.

Collecting stories with a common theme into one volume highlights their repetitive nature and predictability. As soon as a character announces that a new acquaintance "reminds" him of someone, we know that a kinship is to be discovered and the orphan given a home with a hitherto unknown relative. This device, employed in no fewer than eight stories, grows monotonous.

These early stories tend toward sentimentality, didacticism, and predictability but are interesting in that they anticipate strengths to be developed more fully in Montgomery's later fiction. Such strengths include carrying a story forward largely through dialogue, presenting the child's point of view, depicting psychological conflict, and creating a sense of place through concrete details.

Along the Shore: Tales by the Sea

The sixteen stories in *Along the Shore,* collected from periodicals by Rea Wilmshurst and published in 1989, show Montgomery's knowledge of and fondness for the sea. These are, with one exception, representative of early fiction written while she lived in Cavendish, less than a mile from the sea.

As a child, Montgomery spent a great deal of time at the shore, and her observations furnish many of these stories' details. She knew that herring "strike in" during the spring and that the mackerel season begins toward the end of June. The fishermen go out in sailboats to "gib" mackerel,[10] noticing the "odd black streaks" darkening the sea as a sign that the mackerel are beginning to school (*Shore*, 56) and returning at sunset after an 18-hour workday to haul their boats onto skids on the shore. She observed the "faint bleached blue" of the sea in August (*Shore*, 261), the "pearly" insides of mussel shells (*Shore*, 129), and the beacon of a lighthouse glowing dimly through the fog "like a great blur of white mist" (*Shore*, 84).

Several characters in these stories feel the binding power of the sea, and in two the strength of this attachment is the principal plot element. In "The Magical Bond of the Sea," Nora dreams of life beyond her fishing hamlet and willingly goes with a rich couple who wish to adopt her. She is called back by the power of the sea, however, realizing that she belongs not only to life on the shore but to her fisherman lover. In "A Soul That Was Not at Home," a young orphan has a similar experience. Paul leaves the shore to live in town with an adoptive parent who can give him the advantages of books and schooling, only to find that he cannot sleep without the familiar lullaby of the sea "plashing on the rocks" (*Shore*, 134). Feeling imprisoned, the boy returns to the place where the wind, not fettered in the narrow space of the town, can sweep "grandly over great salt waters of the sea" (*Shore*, 136).

The sea has placid and stormy moods, and shoremen know the treachery of its tides and the danger of its sudden squalls. Acts of bravery and daring rescues come at the turning point in half of these stories. The adventure tale was not the type of narrative that Montgomery handled best, but it appealed to readers of juvenile magazines. Two of the rescues have the ironic twist of a man risking his life to save his rival, reminiscent of the Ham-Steerforth episode of *David Copperfield*.

Some of the stories achieve suspense, but most are predictable. In these early stories the author has not yet found her true voice; her skill in portraying the hopes and fears of childhood and her rich sense of the comic rarely appear. Moreover, her weaknesses—including the extensive, adjective-laden passages in praise of the landscape and the grandiloquent language of lovers, especially male lovers—are abundantly evident. Such flaws are most evident in the earliest story, "A Strayed Allegiance," published in *Arthur's Home Magazine* in 1897. This story's action is interrupted by a 119-word description of a sunset, containing 12 color words, 3 similes, 4 metaphors, and some 30 adjectives. Montgomery's favorite color word, "purple," appears and is supplemented by "violet" and "amethystine": truly this is purple prose. The slight and unoriginal plot concerns the high-born Esterbrook Elliott, a name suggesting a character in one of the young Anne's Story Club tales. Esterbrook is betrothed to the lovely Marian, who has a "flower-like face" and wears rosebuds at her throat (*Shore*, 221). All is well, although Marian sometimes feels that her lover's attentions lack "passionate ardour" (*Shore*, 222), until Esterbrook glimpses a fisherman's niece with hair of auburn and gold, a brow of "waxen fairness," and a mouth of "intense crimson" (*Shore*, 225). One look is enough to whiten Esterbrook's face with emotion and to cause the room "to swim before his eyes" (*Shore*, 226). The language he later uses to describe Magdalen to Marian seems typical of a person named Esterbrook: "There was not a shadow of embarrassment in her manner, in spite of the incongruity of her surroundings" (*Shore*, 227). Esterbrook fights a manly battle, torn between passion and honor, and soliloquizes, "Good God, what is this madness that has come over me?" (*Shore*, 231). His honorable manhood wins in the struggle, but Marian, also given to soliloquy, realizes that "the hour of abdication is at hand" (*Shore*, 235), asks to be released from the engagement, and sends Esterbrook to find his tawny Cove girl.

Another story, "A Sandshore Wooing," written in 1913 for *Designer*, is a successful bit of whimsy that demonstrates Montgomery's growing ability as a writer of fiction. When the young female narrator and a male resident at a summer hotel begin to watch each other through spyglasses, the reader is in little doubt of the outcome. Some suspense is provided, however, by the lovers' need to outwit Aunt Martha, who guards her niece from "any horrible attack of a roaring and ravening lion in the disguise of nineteenth-century masculine attire" (*Shore*, 191). The story, composed entirely of excerpts from the heroine's diary, is told in the conversational and often witty manner of the author's own journals. The action moves rapidly, focusing on the romance that develops in spite of Aunt Martha, and contains no digressions describing sunsets or expanses of sea. The humorous courtship is conducted almost entirely from a distance and in the sign language of the deaf, which precludes overly romantic declarations of love.

Again Montgomery used material from these stories in later novels. The imaginative child of "The Soul That Was Not at Home," who has "rock people" as companions, becomes Paul Irving of *Anne of Avonlea*. "The Life-Book of Uncle Jesse" contributes to the portrait of Captain Jim in *Anne's House of Dreams*. In "Four Winds," the rescue of a girl who slips over a cliff while reaching for flowers furnishes an incident for *Emily of New Moon*. The story of "A House Divided against Itself," in which Big George and Little George quarrel over an unclothed statue, finds its way, with few changes, to *A Tangled Web*.

Among the Shadows: Tales from the Darker Side

Although Montgomery generally adopted an optimistic viewpoint and preferred happy endings, her novels provide glimpses of life's mysteries and sorrows. Rea Wilmshurst's 1990 collection of 19 stories focuses on this "darker side" of Montgomery's world view. In these stories, characters steal, get drunk, commit adultery, act in vengeance, and even murder. With only one exception, the author shows compassion for these characters, depicting the factors that led them to break the moral code of their society.

In the six stories dealing with the supernatural, love is a powerful force that reaches out to people from beyond the grave. Montgomery was intrigued by the idea that the dead may communicate with the living, and on one occasion she felt that the unseen spirit of her beloved cousin Frede was in the room with her (*Journals* II, 320). For the most part, however, her attitude seems to have been that of the narrator of "Miriam's Lover," who neither believes nor disbelieves but is willing to "admit the possibility."[11]

The least successful story in the collection is "The Red Room," an early effort published in 1898. Written in stilted language, the tale contains all the elements of Gothic melodrama. On a "fearsome night . . . of storm and blackness" (*Shadows*, 171), in the room that had imprisoned an insane member of the proud Montressor family (shades of Poe), a faithless wife stabs her husband and flees with her foreign lover.

In a later story (1931), the longest in the collection, Montgomery makes an interesting attempt at a detective story, a genre she enjoyed reading in her later years. "Some Fools and a Saint" establishes motives for murder for a closed circle of suspects. Clues are presented fairly, and some real suspense is achieved, but the solution, which uses the device of the "least likely person," is achieved by chance rather than through deduction. Another appealing story is the comic "The Deacon's Painkiller," but most of these tales suffer from their lack of Montgomery's characteristic humor.

In 1911, Montgomery wrote that the short story is a "very high form of art" that presents a greater challenge than the novel (*Journals* II, 36). She wanted to be proficient in this form but was under no illusion about the quality of the majority of her short fiction. "Most of my stories," she admitted, "were written as 'pot-boilers'" (*Journals* II, 36). A few, such as "The Quarantine at Alexander Abraham's" and "Aunt Olivia's Beau," in which she gave free rein to her gift for comedy, are quite entertaining. In most, however, despite evidence of talent, she wrote what she believed would sell and is guilty of hackneyed plots, contrived situations, sentimentality, and didacticism.

Poems

Montgomery's earliest ambition was to be a poet, and she continued to consider poetry a higher form of expression than prose. In 1903, she wrote to MacMillan, "I know that I touch a far higher note in my verse than in prose. But I write much more prose than verse because there is a wider market for it" (*MacMillan*, 3). Most of her poems were written between 1890 and 1915.[12] As she wrote more fiction, she wrote fewer poems but did not abandon her first love, publishing more than 500 poems.

In 1916, Montgomery put together a collection of 94 poems that had previously appeared in 19 different periodicals. The organization of these verses into "Songs of the Sea," "Songs of Hills and Woods," and "Miscellaneous" indicates the predominance of descriptive nature poems in *The Watchman and Other Poems.*

The title poem, "The Watchman," is perhaps Montgomery's most skillful poetic effort. Maximus, a Roman guard at the tomb of Christ, tells a silent listener, Claudia, that meeting the risen Lord has taken away his taste for glory in battle and left him caring only for suffering human beings. He is more ashamed of his reactions than exalted by the experience and hopes that this "weakness" will pass in time. Modeled on the dramatic monologues of Browning, the poem makes the reader aware of the silent audience, Claudia, and of the setting, a garden where "the fountain glitters in the sun among the saffron lilies."[13] The poem is more conversational and less ornate than most Montgomery efforts, and its Browningesque blank verse shows skill in the handling of the pentameter lines and in partial, consonantal rhyme.

Other poems of *The Watchman* volume are less effective because of their ornate diction, archaisms, and repetitious, sometimes awkward, rhymes. In her journals, the writer noted that the poems had no "special merit" but that she had long wanted to produce such a volume for her "own satisfaction" (*Journals* II, 181). When she received the newly published book, she described it as "very nicely gotten up" but added, "I expect no great things of it" (*Journals* II, 194). She was correct in her limited expectations, for the collection received little attention, rather surprisingly in view of her contemporary popularity. It was not reprinted, and today copies are difficult to find. Elizabeth Epperly describes *The Watchman* as a "tame volume" (Epperly, 45), and John Sorfleet comments that some of the verses "are interesting but none are exceptional" (Sorfleet, 5). Frances Frazer finds it a book "that proves how right she was to specialize in prose."[14]

In 1987, John Ferns and Kevin McCabe edited a collection of 86 Montgomery poems, most of these discovered by Rea Wilmshurst in magazines, newspapers, and scrapbooks.[15] The editors disagree with Montgomery's selection of her best verses and include only 17 poems from *The Watchman*.

Montgomery's poetry belongs to the Victorian-Edwardian school of late Romanticism (Ferns, 1986, 29). Her favorite theme is nature as a source of healing and inspiration. Like Wordsworth and his followers, she believed in childhood as a golden age of innocence and natural goodness and preferred the pastoral beauty of the country to the crowded, commercial city. Her sensuous descriptions of natural beauty are in the style of Tennyson and Keats, with liberal use of adjectives, personifications, and similes.

The books of poetry available in the home of Montgomery's grandparents, who considered poetry more suitable reading than novels, clearly influenced her style. The young Montgomery reveled in the works of Tennyson, Whittier, Scott, Byron, Milton, and Burns (*Alpine Path*, 49), and her verse often echoes, consciously or subconsciously, the phraseology of their poetry. A favorite metaphor—that life is a cup of wine to be drained to the lees—is reminiscent of Tennyson's "Ulysses" and Fitzgerald's *Rubaiyat*. She writes "From wandering elf-land bugles far" ("Echo Dell," *Watchman*, 57) in obvious imitation of Tennyson's "Bugle Song," a favorite poem that enthralls both Anne and Emily. When she describes "golden" buttercups "dancing" in the "breeze" ("Buttercups," *Poetry*, 37) and a "dancing host" of poppies ("For Little Things," *Watchman*, 49), there can be no doubt of the influence of Wordsworth's "I Wandered Lonely as a Cloud." Another echo of Wordsworth occurs in the "untrodden ways" of "Rain in the Country" (*Poetry*, 42). The "rare days" of June in "Apple Blossoms" (*Poetry*, 24) recalls Lowell, and the "idle ships" of "Twilight in Abegweit" (*Poetry*, 53) is an image borrowed from Coleridge. "What Children Know" (*Poetry*, 130), a poem in praise of childhood, is obviously indebted to Whittier's "The Barefoot Boy."

In reading through the two collections of Montgomery's verse, one is struck not only by its imitative nature but by its repetitiveness. She was obsessively fond of certain words, including "athwart," "blithesome," "elfin," "minstrelsy," "rainbow," and "wold." She explored all the possibilities of *a* as a prefix, often giving us "afar," "anear," "abrim," "agleam," "adown," "aglitter," and "aquiver." Compound adjectives abound, including "incense-brimmed," "wine-lipped," "sea-girt," and "silver-pinioned." Frequently repeated images include jewels, the moon as a boat, and her favorite image of the cup, which sometimes becomes a "goblet," "flagon," or "chalice." Winds tend to either "pipe" or "keen," the sea to "murmur," and twilight to "creep."

One favorite theme, love of nature, is often expressed in the language of religion,[16] and nature is almost always humanized through personifications. Another favorite theme is a nostalgic longing for home, and several poems reflect, either directly or indirectly, Montgomery's preoccupation with the death of her mother (Ferns, 1986, 36). The short poem "The Wind" illustrates some typical features:

> O, wind! what saw you in the South,
>   In lilied meadows fair and far?
> I saw a lover kiss his lass
>   New-won beneath the evening star.
>
> O, wind! what saw you in the West
>   Of passing sweet that wooed your stay?
> I saw a mother kneeling by
>   The cradle where her first-born lay.
>
> O, wind! what saw you in the North
>   That you shall dream of evermore?
> I saw a maiden keeping tryst
>   Upon a gray and haunted shore.
>
> O, wind! what saw you in the East
>   That still of ancient dole you croon?
> I saw a wan wreck on the waves
>   And a dead face beneath the moon. (*Watchman*, 53)

Although Montgomery used a variety of stanza forms and rhyme schemes, she most frequently wrote in tetrameter lines arranged in four-line stanzas and rhyming ABCB. "The Wind" exemplifies this typical form and her fondness for apostrophe and personification, for associating the sea with danger and death, and for portraying a mother's tenderness. "The Wind" also uses another favorite situation in Montgomery's verse, a woman who must wait while a man goes forth into action and danger. It is not a great poem, but it is technically proficient and has a pleasing ballad quality.

The diction of "The Wind" is less ornate than that of much of Montgomery's verse, where her striving to be poetic resulted in such lines as "And the orient welkin is smit to flame with auroral crimsoning" ("The Voyagers," *Watchman*, 39). Too often she sought the elaborate rather than the simple word, generally preferring "orient" to "east," "welkin" to "sky," "lucent" to "clear," and "portal" to "door."

"The Wind" also lacks the color words so lavishly used in much of the verse and revealing what Montgomery described as her "passionate love of *color*" (*Journals* I, 198). "*Color*," she wrote, "is to me what *music* is to some. I revel in it" (*MacMillan*, 13). Again and again, she used her favorite *purple*, sometimes appropriately but sometimes questionably as in "where the purple noons are long and kind" ("The Call of the Winds," *Watchman*, 83). Six other color words occur in the same 40-line poem. Not all the verses, however, contain vivid colors, for she was almost as fond of "gray" as of "purple" and often wrote of twilight, shadows, and mists.

After her father described an early effort at blank verse as "very blank," the young writer switched to rhyme. To Ephraim Weber she confessed to using a rhyming dictionary and to writing the content of the poem first and then "hunting out rhymes . . . in a very mechanical and cold-blooded fashion" (*Weber*, 34). She has her favorite, often-repeated, rhymes such as "eyes" and "skies," "star" and "far," "up" and "cup," and "dim" and "rim." Sometimes the same rhyming words are used twice in a single poem.

While her ideas and imagery are repetitious, Montgomery's intricate stanza forms and rhyme schemes offer variety. Stanzas vary from 2 to 15 lines in length, and four poems use 11-line stanzas with the challenging rhyme scheme AABCCBDDDEE. She displays technical proficiency in "My Legacy," a series of five tercets using only two rhymes (*Poetry*, 98).

For Montgomery, poetry was distinguished from prose, at least in part, by its conventions. She satirized modern producers of free verse in "I Feel (Vers Libre)," ironically one of her best verses.

> I feel
> Very much
> Like taking
> Its unholy perpetrators
> By the hair
> Of their heads
> (If they have any hair)
> And dragging them around
> A few times,

And then cutting them
Into small, irregular pieces
And burying them
In the depths of the blue sea.
They are without form
And void, / Or at least
The stuff they / produce
Is. / They are too lazy
To hunt up rhymes;
And that
Is all
That is the matter with them. (*Poetry*, 152)

The cleverness displayed in "I Feel (Vers Libre)" appears in
several poems for children, including "The Grumble Family" and
"The Quest of Lazy-Lad." When she attempted light verse, her
natural wit and her facility with feminine rhymes found a hos-
pitable medium. While at Dalhousie College, she won a five-
dollar prize offered by a newspaper for the best letter on the
question "Which has the more patience under the ordinary cares
and trials of life—man or woman?" (*Journals* I, 157) Her entry,
in five six-line stanzas, remains one of her most appealing
poems. "Which Has More Patience—Man or Woman" begins:

As my letter must be brief,
I'll at once state my belief,
And this it is—that, since the world began,
And Adam first did say,
"'Twas Eve led me astray,"
A woman hath more patience than a man. (*Poetry*, 120)

In *The Alpine Path*, Montgomery tells of two great-uncles who
possessed considerable skill in "satirical" and "mock-heroic"
verse (*Alpine Path*, 15). She seems not to have recognized that
her own talent lay in the same area.

Montgomery's verse shows a preference for a male persona
in dramatic poems. In several poems that express a desire for
freedom and that involve men who pursue lives of adventure
and accomplishment while women passively await their return,
the writer may be expressing conscious or subconscious dissatisfaction with the conventional female role.

Although Montgomery never attained great status as a poet, she cannot be written off as a complete failure. Several of her verses have a strong pictorial quality, striking images, and technical facility in difficult forms. Kevin McCabe believes that her verse, frankly designed for a popular audience, has the distinction of "being written with somewhat more talent, individuality, and feeling than the bulk of the verse of its day" and "compares favorably with that of such contemporaries as Pauline Johnson and Robert Service" (McCabe, 18).

Montgomery's reputation as a poet and her success as a short-story writer both suffered from the same affliction: with an eye on the marketplace, she conformed to popular taste. Readers of periodicals liked verses about spring, motherhood, flowers, and the old homeplace, and she supplied, abundantly, what readers and what magazine editors wanted. The didacticism in much of her verse came in response to popular taste, for she disliked "preachy" writing (*Journals* I, 223). Several of her poems are spoiled by a final moralizing stanza tacked on to purely pictorial verses.

Her desire to prove her worth through financial success led Montgomery to overproduce. In 1902, describing recent literary activity, she wrote, "I have ground out several Sunday-Schooly rhymes for a consideration of filthy lucre and I have written one *real* poem out of my heart" (*Journals* I, 279). In connection with this catering to the popular market, both in her verses and in her short stories, one poem, "The Test" (*Poetry*, 115), seems particularly significant. The first two stanzas describe the "thunderous applause" given to a playwright by an audience but the failure of one spectator, "the Artist," to approve. The poem concludes:

> It was he,
> He, the master, I strove to please.
> Naught had my hope availed,
> That grim old veteran of victories
> Was silent . . . I had failed.

Afterword

When Montgomery wrote for the child within herself, she struck a responsive chord in the hearts of readers of all ages. She convincingly portrayed imaginative and sensitive children striving to come to terms with a world dominated by adults.

Unfortunately, she never left behind her the insecure child who was constantly made to feel inferior, and this detracted from the quality of her writing. Her obsessive desire to please prompted her to write what she believed would gain the approval of her relatives, her associates, her husband's parishioners, her editors, and her reading public. Too often, she went against her own preferences and talents to seek popularity. In addition, Montgomery felt that her world measured success in terms of money and was determined to establish herself financially. To prove her worth to her money-conscious society and to herself, she overproduced, frequently resorting to stale plot contrivances and repetitive characters and situations.

Montgomery has nevertheless won a secure place among writers who have special appeal for children not by breaking patterns but by using them more effectively than most of her predecessors and contemporaries. She rehabilitated the orphan novel, a tradition with long and proven appeal, by reducing its customary sentimentality and religiosity and by creating believable protagonists who are appealingly honest and not always well behaved. She used the stereotypes of the orphan heroine and the literary heroine to develop her favorite theme—the idiosyncratic child who seeks to establish her identity and find her place. This quest for identity and belonging remains a dominant theme in contemporary books for and about the young. The tougher, more audacious Gilly Hopkins and Harriet the Spy, creations of Katherine Paterson and Louise Fitzhugh, may seem a far cry from Anne and Emily, but they are essentially of the same breed.

Although she was bound by the conventions of her age, some elements of Montgomery's works are surprisingly modern. She adopted the Romantic-Victorian-Edwardian view of childhood as the age of innocence and natural goodness yet created such unpleasant specimens of children as Josie Pye and Rhoda Stuart. The lives of all her young protagonists are darkened by encounters with fear, death, loneliness, and injustice as they travel "the golden road." Moreover, contrary to Victorian ideals, her children are self-reliant and challenge the wisdom of their adult mentors (Townsend, 89). The "subversive" doctrine of *Anne of Green Gables* continues to the present in children's literature, as does Montgomery's depiction of child-adult conflicts.

The regional idyll dominated Canadian fiction during the first two decades of the twentieth century.[1] Again, Montgomery was part of the popular trend, but her rural Edens were less idealistic than those of most regionalists. Her country villages are not without narrow-mindedness, prejudice, hypocrisy, and petty malice. There are "pigsties" among the "pine woods," even in Avonlea.

Montgomery accepted a Victorian tenet that stories for girls must idealize woman's conventional role as homemaker and nurturer, but she followed it with grace and humor. Her novels, especially the Emily trilogy, contain evidence that she was uneasy with the requirement.

Sentimentality and didacticism have passed out of favor, although the modern problem novel for young adults usually has a message and can be didactic in its own way. When Montgomery wrote, sentimentality and didacticism were not only acceptable but expected in stories for girls. She did not defy popular taste, but her sense of humor usually saved her from the blatant use of either feature, at least in her novels. She even satirizes both tendencies in *Anne of Green Gables*. Of the commercial necessity of "dragging in a moral" she wrote: "The kind of juvenile story I like best to write—and read, too, for the matter of that—is a good, jolly one, 'art for art's sake,' or rather 'fun for fun's sake,' with no insidious moral hidden away in it like a pill in a spoonful of jam!" (*Alpine Path*, 62).

Literature for children and young adults has developed in some directions that Montgomery either could not or did not choose to take. Today the child dealing with the problems of being different often belongs to a minority group, whereas Montgomery's viewpoint is always that of the white Anglo-Saxon Protestant. Taboos have been lifted; literature for the young now addresses sexuality, pregnancy, drugs, divorce, and racial unrest. Problems are not always solved, and endings are not always happy, reflecting a more honest if less optimistic view of life. Perhaps this harsh honesty and social relevance explain the revival of interest in Montgomery's work. Young readers may welcome an escape to a more secure world where things turn out for the best.

Montgomery disliked didacticism, and she regretted that she did not write honestly of young girlhood, that her heroines, after leaving childhood, were "sweet, insipid" beings "to whom the basic realities of life and reactions . . . are quite unknown" (*MacMillan,* 118). Through her critic-characters—Mr. Carpenter, Mr. Harrison, and Captain Jim—she deplores the dishonesty of happily-ever-after endings and lengthy romantic scenes characterized by overblown diction. These critics also warn against consciously poetic language and long descriptive passages that interrupt the action. Nevertheless, eager for acceptance and popularity, Montgomery often was caught in these snares. We will never know what she might have written had she not been conditioned by her restrictive upbringing and unfortunate marriage to seek approval rather than independence.[2] Her talents are impressive and undeniable. Her strong sense of the comic, aptitude for dialogue, ability to create a sense of place, and precise recall of how it feels to be a child are outstanding. These qualities have ensured the continuing popularity that she so much desired.

Notes and References

Chapter One

1. *My Dear Mr. M: Letters to G. B. MacMillan*, ed. Francis W. P. Bolger and Elizabeth R. Epperly (Toronto: McGraw-Hill Ryerson, 1980), 115; hereafter cited in text as *MacMillan*.

2. *The Selected Journals of L. M. Montgomery, Volume II: 1910–1921*, ed. Mary Rubio and Elizabeth Waterston (Toronto: Oxford University Press, 1987), 67; hereafter cited in text as *Journals* II.

3. *The Alpine Path: The Story of My Career* (Don Mills, Ontario: Fitzhenry and Whiteside, 1974; copyright L. M. Montgomery, 1917), 18; hereafter cited in text as *Alpine Path*.

4. *The Selected Journals of L. M. Montgomery, Volume I: 1889–1910*, ed. Mary Rubio and Elizabeth Waterston (Toronto: Oxford University Press, 1985), 375; hereafter cited in text as *Journals* I.

5. Elizabeth Waterston, "Lucy Maud Montgomery, 1874–1942," *Canadian Children's Literature* 1.3 (1975): 10; hereafter cited in text as Waterston.

6. Mollie Gillen, *Lucy Maud Montgomery* (Don Mills, Ontario: Fitzhenry and Whiteside, 1978), 17; hereafter cited in text as Gillen, 1978.

7. *The Green Gables Letters from L. M. Montgomery to Ephraim Weber 1905–1909*, ed. Wilfred Eggleston (Ottawa: Borealis, 1981), 35; hereafter cited in text as *Weber*.

8. Margaret Mustard, *L. M. Montgomery as Mrs. Ewan Macdonald of Leaskdale Manse 1911–1926* (Leaskdale, Ontario: St. Paul's Presbyterian Women's Association, 1965), 2; hereafter cited in text as Mustard.

9. *Rainbow Valley* (New York: A. L. Burt, 1919), 163.

10. Mollie Gillen, *The Wheel of Things: A Biography of L. M. Montgomery* (Halifax, Nova Scotia: Formac, 1983), 152; hereafter cited in text as Gillen, 1983.

11. John R. Sorfleet, "L. M. Montgomery: Canadian Authoress," *Canadian Children's Literature* 1.3 (1975): 6; hereafter cited in text as Sorfleet.

Chapter Two

1. *The Alpine Path*, 72. In a journal entry for 16 August 1907, Montgomery gives a later date for the beginning (May 1905) and completion (January 1906) but may be referring to the revisions made before sending the manuscript to Page. Biographers have accepted the dates given in *The Alpine Path*.

2. Again, there is a slight discrepancy between the account given in the autobiography and in the journals. The autobiography gives the number of rejections as five, whereas the journals mention only four.

3. *Anne of Green Gables* (New York: Bantam, 1976), 1; hereafter cited in text as *AGG*.

4. Jon C. Stott, "L. M. Montgomery," in *Writers for Children*, ed. Jane M. Bingham (New York: Charles Scribner's, 1988), 418; hereafter cited in text as Stott.

5. Mary Rubio, "'Anne of Green Gables': The Architect of Adolescence," in *Touchstones: Reflections on the Best in Children's Literature*, Vol. 1, ed. Perry Nodelman (West Lafayette, Indiana: Children's Literature Association, 1985), 176; hereafter cited in text as Rubio, 1985.

6. Elizabeth Waterston and Mary Rubio, "Afterword," in *Anne of Green Gables* (New York: New American Library, 1987), 312–13; hereafter cited in text as Waterston and Rubio, 1987; *AGG*. Although I have made minor alterations, I am indebted to the plot outline by Waterston and Rubio.

7. Susan Drain, "'Too Much Love-Making': *Anne of Green Gables* on Television," *The Lion and the Unicorn* 11.2 (October 1987): 64; hereafter cited in text as Drain.

8. Rachel Carson, *The Sense of Wonder* (New York: Harper & Row, 1964), 43.

9. William Wordsworth, "Lines Composed a Few Miles above Tintern Abbey," 1.85.

10. Allan Bloom, *Closing of the American Mind* (New York: Simon and Schuster, 1987), 141.

11. Coleridge, *Biographia Literaria*, XIII.

12. Coleridge, "Dejection: An Ode," 1.86.

13. Susan Drain, "Community and the Individual in *Anne of Green Gables*: The Meaning of Belonging," *Children's Literature Association Quarterly* 11.1 (1986): 19.

14. Carol Gay, "'Kindred Spirits' All: Green Gables Revisited," *Children's Literature Association Quarterly* 11.1 (1986): 11.

15. Muriel A. Whitaker, "'Queer Children': L. M. Montgomery's Heroines," *Canadian Children's Literature* 1.3 (Autumn 1975): 51; hereafter cited in text as Whitaker.

16. Alison Lurie, *Don't Tell the Grown-ups: Subversive Children's Literature* (Boston: Little, Brown, 1990). Lurie contends that most classics of children's literature tend to be "subversive" in the sense that they criticize adult conventions and pretensions.

17. Eudora Welty, "Place in Fiction," in *The Eye of the Story: Selected Essays and Reviews* (New York: Vintage, 1979), 118.

18. Marilyn Solt, "The Uses of Setting in *Anne of Green Gables*," *Children's Literature Association Quarterly* 9.4 (Winter 1984–85): 179, 180, 198. I am indebted to Solt for calling attention to several of the details used in my discussion of setting but have omitted some of those in her essay and added a few of my own.

19. T. D. MacLulich, "L. M. Montgomery and the Literary Heroine: Jo, Rebecca, Anne, and Emily," *Canadian Children's Literature* 37 (1985): 11; hereafter cited in text as MacLulich, 1985, "Heroine."

20. Mary Rubio, "Satire, Realism, and Imagination in *Anne of Green Gables*," *Canadian Children's Literature* 1.3 (Autumn 1975): 31.

21. John Rowe Townsend, *Written for Children* (London: Penguin, 1974), 34; hereafter cited in text as Townsend.

22. Frank Luther Mott, *Golden Multitudes: The Story of Best Sellers in the United States* (New York: R. R. Bowker, 1947), 216.

23. Gillian Avery, "'Remarkable and Winning': A Hundred Years of American Heroines," *The Lion and the Unicorn* 13.1 (June 1989): 17; hereafter cited in text as Avery.

24. The letter from Twain (3 October 1908) is partially quoted in a letter to Weber (*Green Gables Letters*, 80) and is frequently cited by biographers and critics.

25. Sheila Egoff, *The Republic of Childhood: A Critical Guide to Canadian Children's Literature in English* (Toronto: Oxford University Press, 1967), 249, 252.

26. Ruth Weber Russell, D. W. Russell, and Rea Wilmshurst, *Lucy Maud Montgomery: A Preliminary Bibliography* (Waterloo, Ontario: University of Waterloo Library, 1986), 10. Some sources give the number of translations as considerably higher than 16. An editorial note in the Bantam edition of *Further Chronicles of Avonlea* states that there have been 36 translations.

27. Jonathan Cott, "The Astonishment of Being," *New Yorker*, 29 February 1983, 57.

28. Barbara Wachowicz, "L. M. Montgomery: At Home in Poland," *Canadian Children's Literature* 46 (1987): 9; hereafter cited in text as Wachowicz.

29. Yuko Katsura, "Red-haired Anne in Japan," *Canadian Children's Literature* 34 (1984): 58.

30. Charmaine Gaudet, "Why the Japanese Love Our *Anne of Green Gables*," *Canadian Geographic*, February/March 1987, 13; hereafter cited in text as Gaudet.

31. Quoted in Gillen, 1983, 79. This letter from Montgomery to Murray Macneill, dated July 1909, is in the possession of John Macneill of Cavendish.

32. Jacqueline Berke, "Mother, I Can Do It Myself: The Self-sufficient Heroine in Popular Girls' Fiction," *Women's Studies* 6.2 (1979): 197; hereafter cited in text as Berke.

33. Brian D. Johnson, Barbara MacAndrew, and Ann Shortell, "Anne of Green Gables Grows Up," *Maclean's*, 7 December 1987, 47.

Chapter Three

1. *Anne of Avonlea* (New York: Grosset and Dunlap, 1936), 118–21; hereafter cited in text as *AA*.

2. Elizabeth Waterston and Mary Rubio, "Afterword," in *Anne of Avonlea* (New York: New American Library, 1987), 275; hereafter cited in text as Waterston and Rubio, 1987; *AA*.

3. I am indebted to Waterston and Rubio for their calling attention to the "explosions" occurring in *Anne of Avonlea*.

4. *Anne of the Island* (New York: Grosset and Dunlap, 1915),18; hereafter cited in text as *AI*.

5. Mary Rubio and Elizabeth Waterston, eds., *Selected Journals of L. M. Montgomery* I, 406 (note on journal entry of 14 March 1896).

6. *Anne's House of Dreams* (New York: Grosset and Dunlap, 1917), 31; hereafter cited in text as *AHD*.

7. Gillian Thomas, "The Decline of Anne: Matron vs. Child," *Canadian Children's Literature* 1.3 (Autumn 1975): 40; hereafter cited in text as Thomas.

8. T. D. MacLulich, "L. M. Montgomery's Portraits of the Artist: Realism, Idealism, and the Domestic Imagination," *English Studies in Canada* 11.4 (1985): 471–72; hereafter cited in text as MacLulich, 1985, "Portraits."

9. Elizabeth Waterston and Mary Rubio, "Afterword," in *Anne's House of Dreams* (New York: New American Library, 1989), 282.

10. Elizabeth Epperly, "L. M. Montgomery's *Anne's House of Dreams*: Reworking Poetry," *Canadian Children's Literature* 37 (1985): 41; hereafter cited in text as Epperly.

Chapter Four

1. Rosamond Bailey, "Little Orphan Mary: Anne's Hoydenish Double," *Canadian Children's Literature* 55 (1989): 8; hereafter cited in text as Bailey.

2. *Rainbow Valley* (New York: A.L. Burt, 1919), 16; hereafter cited in text as *RV*.

3. *Rilla of Ingleside* (New York: Frederick A. Stokes, 1921), 112–13; hereafter cited in text as *RI*.

4. Helen Porter, "The Fair World of L. M. Montgomery," *Journal of Canadian Fiction* 2.4 (1973): 102; hereafter cited in text as Porter.

5. Carol Gaboury, "L. M. Montgomery, Poet," *Kindred Spirits* 4 (1989): 6; hereafter cited in text as Gaboury.

6. Margery Fee and Ruth Cawker, *Canadian Fiction: An Annotated Bibliography* (Toronto: Peter Martin Associates, 1976), 79.

7. *Anne of Windy Poplars* (New York: Pocket Books, 1940), 14; hereafter cited in text as *AWP*.

8. *Anne of Ingleside* (New York: Grosset and Dunlap, 1939), 1; hereafter cited in text as *AIng*.

9. Jean Little, "But What about Jane?" *Canadian Children's Literature* 1.3 (Autumn 1975): 71; hereafter cited in text as Little.

10. Ann S. Cowan, "Canadian Writers: Lucy Maud and Emily Byrd," *Canadian Children's Literature* 1.3 (Autumn 1975): 43.

Chapter Five

1. *Emily of New Moon* (New York: Grosset and Dunlap, 1923), 14; hereafter cited in text as *ENM*.

2. Judith Miller, "The Writer-as-a-Young-Woman and Her Family: Montgomery's Emily," *New Quarterly: New Directions in Canadian Writing* 7.1, 2 (Spring–Summer 1987): 306; hereafter cited in text as Miller, 1987.

3. Thomas E. Tausky, "L. M. Montgomery and 'The Alpine Path, So Hard, So Steep,'" *Canadian Children's Literature* 30 (1983): 10; hereafter cited in text as Tausky.

4. *Emily Climbs* (New York: Frederick A. Stokes, 1925), 179–82; hereafter cited in text as *EC*.

5. Judith Miller, "Montgomery's Emily: Voices and Silences," *Studies in Canadian Literature* 9.2 (1984): 163; hereafter cited in text as Miller, 1984.

6. Montgomery to Ephraim Weber, 18 July 1926; in Tausky, 15.

7. *Emily's Quest* (New York: Grosset and Dunlap, 1927), 33; hereafter cited in text as *EQ*.

Chapter Six

1. *The Story Girl* (Boston: L. C. Page, 1911), 124; hereafter cited in text as *SG*.

2. Joyce-Ione Harrington Coldwell, "Folklore as Fiction: The Writings of L. M. Montgomery" in *Folklore Studies in Honor of Herbert Halpert*, ed. Kenneth S. Goldstein and Neil V. Rosenberg (St. John's, Newfoundland: Memorial University of Newfoundland, 1980), 125; hereafter cited in text as Coldwell.

3. Interview with Mrs. John Macneill, August 1987.

4. *The Golden Road* (Boston: L. C. Page, 1913), vii; hereafter cited in text as *GR*.

5. *Pat of Silver Bush* (New York: Grosset and Dunlap, 1933), 7; hereafter cited in text as *PSB*.

6. *Mistress Pat* (New York: Grosset and Dunlap, 1935), 28; hereafter cited in text as *MP*.

7. Jane Cowan Fredeman, "The Land of Lost Content: The Use of Fantasy in L. M. Montgomery's Novels," *Canadian Children's Literature* 1.3 (Autumn 1975): 66; hereafter cited in text as Fredeman.

Chapter Seven

1. *Kilmeny of the Orchard* (New York; Grosset and Dunlap, 1910), 212; hereafter cited in text as *KO*.

2. *The Blue Castle* (Toronto: McClelland-Bantam, 1988), 21; hereafter cited in text as *BC*.

3. Reviews from *New York World* and *Literary Review*, *Book Review Digest* (1926): 492.

4. Chris Wood, Philip Grenard, and Barbara MacAndrew, "A Tale of Twin Spinsters," *Maclean's*, 15 February 1988, 59.

5. *Magic for Marigold* (New York: A.L. Burt, 1929), 34; hereafter cited in text as *MM*.

6. *A Tangled Web* (New York: Frederick A. Stokes, 1931), 139; hereafter cited in text as *TW*.

7. *Jane of Lantern Hill* (New York: Grosset and Dunlap, 1937), 42; hereafter cited in text as *JLH*.

Chapter Eight

1. Catherine McLay, "Introduction," *The Doctor's Sweetheart and Other Stories* (Toronto: McGraw-Hill Ryerson, 1979), 4; hereafter cited in text as McLay.

2. *Chronicles of Avonlea* (New York: Grosset and Dunlap, 1940), 64; hereafter cited in text as *CA*.

3. Mary Jane Edwards, Paul Denham, and George Parker, eds., *The Evolution of Canadian Literature in English: 1867–1914* (Toronto: Holt, Rinehart & Winston of Canada, 1973), 314.

4. *Further Chronicles of Avonlea* (Toronto: McClelland-Bantam, 1987), 16.

5. Publisher's Foreword, *The Road to Yesterday* (Toronto: McGraw-Hill Ryerson, 1974).

6. *The Road to Yesterday* (Toronto: McGraw-Hill Ryerson, 1974), 87.

7. *The Doctor's Sweetheart and Other Stories*, ed. Catherine McLay (Toronto: McGraw-Hill Ryerson, 1979), 107; hereafter cited in text as *DS*.

8. Rea Wilmshurst, "Introduction," *Akin to Anne: Tales of Other Orphans* (Toronto: McClelland and Stewart, 1988), 7–8; hereafter cited in text as Wilmshurst.

9. *Akin to Anne: Tales of Other Orphans*, ed. Rea Wilmshurst (Toronto: McClelland and Stewart, 1988), 15–17; hereafter cited in text as *Akin*.

10. *Along the Shore: Tales by the Sea*, ed. Rea Wilmshurst (Toronto: McClelland and Stewart, 1989), 57; hereafter cited in text as *Shore*.

11. *Among the Shadows: Tales from the Darker Side*, ed. Rea Wilmshurst (New York: Bantam, 1991), 123; hereafter cited in text as *Shadows*.

12. John Ferns, "'Rainbow Dreams': The Poetry of Lucy Maud Montgomery," *Canadian Children's Literature* 42 (1986): 30; hereafter cited in text as Ferns.

13. *The Watchman and Other Poems* (New York: Frederick A. Stokes, 1917), 3; hereafter cited in text as *Watchman*.

14. Frances M. Frazer, "Island Writers," *Canadian Literature* 68–69 (1976): 82.

15. John Ferns and Kevin McCabe, *The Poetry of Lucy Maud Montgomery* (Markham, Ontario: Fitzhenry and Whiteside, 1987); hereafter cited in text as *Poetry*.

16. Kevin McCabe, "Introduction," *The Poetry of Lucy Maud Montgomery* (Markham, Ontario: Fitzhenry and Whiteside, 1987), 4; hereafter cited in text as McCabe.

Afterword

1. Desmond Pacey, *Creative Writing in Canada* (Toronto: McGraw-Hill Ryerson, 1961), 102.

2. Janice Kulyk Keefer, *Under Eastern Eyes: A Critical Reading of Maritime Fiction* (Toronto: University of Toronto Press, 1987), 250.

Selected Bibliography

PRIMARY WORKS

Novels

Anne of Green Gables. Boston: L. C. Page, 1908.
Anne of Avonlea. Boston: L. C. Page, 1909.
Kilmeny of the Orchard. Boston: L. C. Page, 1910.
The Story Girl. Boston: L. C. Page, 1911.
The Golden Road. Boston: L. C. Page, 1913.
Anne of the Island. Boston: L. C. Page, 1915.
Anne's House of Dreams. New York: Frederick Stokes, 1917.
Rainbow Valley. New York: Frederick Stokes, 1919.
Rilla of Ingleside. New York: Frederick Stokes, 1921.
Emily of New Moon. New York: Frederick Stokes, 1923.
Emily Climbs. New York: Frederick Stokes, 1925.
The Blue Castle. New York: Frederick Stokes, 1926.
Emily's Quest. New York: Frederick Stokes, 1927.
Magic for Marigold. New York: Frederick Stokes, 1929.
A Tangled Web. New York: Frederick Stokes, 1931.
Pat of Silver Bush. New York: Frederick Stokes, 1933.
Mistress Pat. New York: Frederick Stokes, 1935.
Anne of Windy Poplars. New York: Frederick Stokes, 1936.
Jane of Lantern Hill. New York: Frederick Stokes, 1937.
Anne of Ingleside. New York: Frederick Stokes, 1939.

Stories and Verse

Chronicles of Avonlea. Boston: L. C. Page, 1912.
The Watchman and Other Poems. Toronto: McClelland and Stewart, 1916.
Further Chronicles of Avonlea. Boston: L. C. Page, 1920.
The Road to Yesterday. Toronto: McGraw-Hill Ryerson, 1974.

The Doctor's Sweetheart and Other Stories. Edited by Catherine McLay. Toronto: McGraw-Hill Ryerson, 1979.

The Poetry of Lucy Maud Montgomery. Selected and introduced by John Ferns and Kevin McCabe. Markham, Ontario: Fitzhenry and Whiteside, 1987.

Akin to Anne: Tales of Other Orphans. Edited by Rea Wilmshurst. Toronto: McClelland and Stewart, 1988.

Along the Shore: Tales by the Sea. Edited by Rea Wilmshurst. Toronto: McClelland and Stewart, 1989.

Among the Shadows: Tales from the Darker Side. Edited by Rea Wilmshurst. Toronto: McClelland and Stewart, 1990.

Other

The Alpine Path: The Story of My Career. Don Mills, Ontario: Fitzhenry and Whiteside, 1974. Copyright L. M. Montgomery 1917. An autobiographical sketch, originally published in *Everywoman's World*, that focuses on the author's childhood in Cavendish and her success with *Anne of Green Gables*. Presents optimistic viewpoint without reference to personal frustrations.

Courageous Women. Toronto: McClelland and Stewart, 1934. Biographical sketches written in collaboration with Marian Keith and Mabel Burns McKinley.

My Dear Mr. M: Letters to G. B. MacMillan. Edited by Francis W. P. Bolger and Elizabeth R. Epperly. Toronto: McGraw-Hill Ryerson, 1980. Letters of Montgomery to her Scottish friend cover the period from 1903 to her final illness and are invaluable for knowledge of her personal and professional life.

The Green Gables Letters from L. M. Montgomery to Ephraim Weber 1905–1909. Edited by Wilfred Eggleston. 2d ed. Ottawa: Borealis, 1981. Letters to a Canadian friend from the period of the composition and publication of *Anne of Green Gables*.

The Selected Journals of L. M. Montgomery, Volume I: 1889–1910. Edited by Mary Rubio and Elizabeth Waterston. Toronto: Oxford University Press, 1985. Selections from the first two of ten handwritten journals cover Montgomery's life from ages 14 to 36. Well annotated with a helpful introduction.

The Selected Journals of L. M. Montgomery, Volume II: 1910–1921. Edited by Mary Rubio and Elizabeth Waterston. Toronto: Oxford University Press, 1987. Selections from the journals dealing principally with the Leaskdale years. This and the previous volume are the best source for understanding the author's personal and literary life. Useful notes and introduction.

SECONDARY WORKS

Books, Parts of Books, and Monographs

Bolger, Francis W. P. *The Years before "Anne".* Charlottetown: Prince Edward Island Heritage Foundation, 1974. An account of Montgomery's life prior to her publication of *Anne of Green Gables.* Contains letters and examples of early writing not published elsewhere.

Coldwell, Joyce-Ione Harrington. "Folklore as Fiction: The Writings of L. M. Montgomery." In *Folklore Studies in Honor of Herbert Halpert,* edited by Kenneth S. Goldstein and Neil V. Rosenberg, 125–36. St. John's, Newfoundland: Memorial University of Newfoundland, 1980.

Edwards, Mary Jane, Paul Denham, and George Parker, eds. *The Evolution of Canadian Literature in English,* 313–15. Toronto: Holt, Rinehart, and Winston of Canada, 1973.

Gillen, Mollie. *Lucy Maud Montgomery.* Don Mills, Ontario: Fitzhenry and Whiteside, 1978. A short account, for young readers, of Montgomery's life.

_____. *The Wheel of Things.* Don Mills, Ontario: Fitzhenry and Whiteside, 1975. Paperback reprint Halifax, Nova Scotia: Formac, 1983. Highly readable and the best biography to date. Unfortunately omits sources of quotations.

Keefer, Janice Kulyk. *Under Eastern Eyes: A Critical Reading of Maritime Fiction.* Toronto: University of Toronto Press, 1987.

Kensinger, Faye R. *Chil..en of the Series and How They Grew.* Bowling Green, Ohio: Bowling Green State University Popular Press, 1987.

MacLulich, T. D. *Between Europe and America: The Canadian Tradition in Fiction.* Oakville: ECW Press, 1988.

Mott, Frank Luther. *Golden Multitudes: The Story of Best Sellers in the United States.* New York: R. R. Bowker, 1947.

Mustard, Maud. *L. M. Montgomery as Mrs. Ewan Macdonald of the Leaskdale Manse, 1911–1926.* Leaskdale, Ontario: St. Paul's Presbyterian Woman's Association, 1965. Laudatory anecdotes supplied by members of the Leaskdale congregation.

Ridley, Hilda M. *The Story of L. M. Montgomery.* Foreword by M. M. Mitchell. Toronto: Ryerson Press, 1956. First book-length biography. Noncritical and lavish with praise. Emphasizes effect of Montgomery's childhood on writing.

Rubio, Mary. "'Anne of Green Gables': The Architect of Adolescence." In *Touchstones: Reflections on the Best in Children's Literature,* vol. 1, edited by Perry Nodelman, 173–87. West Lafayette, Indiana: Children's Literature Association, 1985.

Russell, Ruth Weber, D. W. Russell, and Rea Wilmshurst. *Lucy Maud Montgomery: A Preliminary Bibliography*. Waterloo, Ontario: University of Waterloo Library, 1986.

Stott, Jon C. "L. M. Montgomery." In *Writers for Children*, edited by Jane M. Bingham, 415–22. New York: Charles Scribners Sons, 1988.

Sorfleet, John. "L. M. Montgomery." In *Twentieth Century Children's Writers*, edited by D. L. Kirkpatrick, 553–55. New York: St. Martin's Press, 1983.

_____, ed. *L. M. Montgomery: An Assessment*. Guelph, Ontario: Canadian Children's Press, 1976. A monograph reprint of articles in *Canadian Children's Literature* 1.3 (Autumn 1975).

Townsend, John Rowe. *Written for Children*. London: Penguin Books, 1974.

Waterston, Elizabeth. "Lucy Maud Montgomery." In *The Clear Spirit: Twenty Canadian Women and Their Times*, edited by Mary Quayle, Innis, 198–220. Toronto: University of Toronto Press, 1966. Reprinted in *Canadian Children's Literature* 1.3 (1975) and in *L. M. Montgomery: An Assessment*, edited by John R. Sorfleet, Guelph: Canadian Children's Press, 1976. A concise and effective overview of the life and works of Montgomery.

Articles

Avery, Gillian. "'Remarkable and Winning': A Hundred Years of American Heroines." *The Lion and the Unicorn* 13.1 (1989): 7–20.

Bailey, Rosamond. "Little Orphan Mary: Anne's Hoydenish Double." *Canadian Children's Literature* 55 (1989): 8–17.

Berke, Jacqueline. "'Mother, I can do it myself!': The Self-sufficient Heroine in Popular Girls' Fiction." *Women's Studies* 6.2 (1979): 187–203.

Cowan, Ann S. "Canadian Writers: Lucy Maud and Emily Byrd." *Canadian Children's Literature* 1.3 (1975): 42–49. Reprinted in *L. M. Montgomery: An Assessment*, edited by John P. Sorfleet.

Drain, Susan. "Community and the Individual in *Anne of Green Gables:* The Meaning of Belonging." *Children's Literature Association Quarterly* 11.1 (1986): 15–19.

_____. "'Too Much Love-making': *Anne of Green Gables* on Television." *The Lion and the Unicorn* 11.2 (1987): 63–72.

Epperly, Elizabeth P. "L. M. Montgomery's *Anne's House of Dreams*: Reworking Poetry." *Canadian Children's Literature* 37 (1985): 40–45.

Ferns, John. "'Rainbow Dreams': The Poetry of Lucy Maud Montgomery." *Canadian Children's Literature* 42 (1986): 29–40.

Frazer, Frances M. "Island Writers." *Canadian Literature* 68–69 (1976): 76–87.

Fredeman, Jane Cowan. "The Land of Lost Content: The Use of Fantasy in L. M. Montgomery's Novels." *Canadian Children's Literature* 1.3 (1975): 60–70. Reprinted in *L. M. Montgomery: An Assessment*, edited by John R. Sorfleet.

Gaudet, Charmaine. "Why the Japanese Love Our *Anne of Green Gables*." *Canadian Geographic* 107.1 (1987): 8–14.

Gay, Carol. "'Kindred Spirits' All: Green Gables Revisited." *Children's Literature Association Quarterly* 11.1 (1986): 9–12.

Hill, Maude Petitt. "The Best Known Woman in Prince Edward Island, L. M. Montgomery, Author of *Anne of Green Gables*." *Chatelaine*, May 1988, 8–9, 65; June 1928, 23, 41–42.

Katsura, Yuko. "Red-Haired Anne in Japan." *Canadian Children's Literature* 34 (1984): 57–60.

Little, Jean. "But What about Jane?" *Canadian Children's Literature* 1.3 (1975): 71–81. Reprinted in *L. M. Montgomery: An Assessment*, edited by John R. Sorfleet.

McCabe, Kevin. "Lucy Maud Montgomery: The Person and the Poet." *Canadian Children's Literature* 38 (1985): 68–80.

MacLulich, T. D. "L. M. Montgomery and the Literary Heroine: Jo, Rebecca, Anne, and Emily." *Canadian Children's Literature* 37 (1985): 5–17.

_____. "L. M. Montgomery's Portraits of the Artist: Realism, Idealism, and the Domestic Imagination." *English Studies in Canada* 11.4 (1985): 459–73.

Miller, Judith. "Montgomery's Emily: Voices and Silences." *Studies in Canadian Literature* 9.2 (1984): 158–68.

_____. "The Writer-as-a-young-woman and Her Family: Montgomery's Emily." *The New Quarterly* 7.1–2 (1987): 301–19.

Porter, Helen. "The Fair World of L. M. Montgomery." *Journal of Canadian Fiction* 2.4 (1973): 102–4.

Rubio, Mary. "Satire, Realism, and Imagination in *Anne of Green Gables*." *Canadian Children's Literature* 1.3 (1975): 27–36. Reprinted in *L. M. Montgomery: An Assessment*, edited by John R. Sorfleet.

Solt, Marilyn. "The Uses of Setting in *Anne of Green Gables.*" *Children's Literature Association Quarterly* 9.4 (1984–1985): 179–80, 198.

Sorfleet, John R. "L. M. Montgomery: Canadian Authoress." *Canadian Children's Literature* 1.3 (1975): 4–7. Reprinted in *L. M. Montgomery: An Assessment*, edited by John R. Sorfleet.

Tausky, Thomas E. "L. M. Montgomery and 'The Alpine Path, so hard, so steep.'" *Canadian Children's Literature* 30 (1983): 5–20.

Thomas, Gillian. "The Decline of Anne: Matron vs. Child." *Canadian Children's Literature* 1.3 (1975): 37–41. Reprinted in *L. M. Montgomery: An Assessment*, edited by John R. Sorfleet.

Wachowicz, Barbara. "L. M. Montgomery: At Home in Poland." *Canadian Children's Literature* 46 (1987): 7–36.

Weale, David. "'No Scope for Imagination': Another Side of *Anne of Green Gables.*" *The Island* 20 (1986): 3–8.

Weber, E. "L. M. Montgomery's 'Anne.'" *Dalhousie Review* 24 (1944): 64–73.

Whitaker, Muriel A. "'Queer Children': L. M. Montgomery's Heroines." *Canadian Children's Literature* 1.3 (1975): 50–59. Reprinted in *L. M. Montgomery: An Assessment*, edited by John R. Sorfleet.

Index

The Author

Genevieve Wiggins, a professor of English at Tennessee Wesleyan College, received her B.A. from the University of Chattanooga, her M.A. from Vanderbilt University, and her Ph.D. from the University of Tennessee. She has written several articles on the history and folklore of East Tennessee and is coeditor and contributing author of two books on local history. She has had a lifelong interest in the works of L. M. Montgomery.